M000276301

LIKE

AN

OCEAN

VOLUME I
LENT AND EASTER

REV. FR. JOSEPH OKINE-QUARTEY (PH.D)

Like An Ocean
Volume I
Lent and Easter

Copyright © 2021 by Rev. Fr. Joseph Okine-Quartey (Ph.D).

Paperback ISBN: 978-1-63812-040-7
Hardcover ISBN: 978-1-63812-042-1
Ebook ISBN: 978-1-63812-041-4

All rights reserved. No part in this book may be produced and transmitted in any form or by any means, electronic, or mechanical, including photocopying, recording, or by any information storage and retrieval system, without permission in writing from the copyright owner.

The views expressed in this work are solely those of the author and do not necessarily reflect the views of the publisher hereby disclaims any responsibility for them.

Published by Green Sage Agency   05/27/2021

Green Sage Agency
1-888-366-9989
inquiry@greensageagency.com

To
The Parishioners of
St. John the Baptist Plum City, WI
St. Joseph Arkansaw, WI
St. Thomas Aquinas, UG, Legon, Accra
And
St. Paul's Catholic Seminary, Sowutuom, Accra

FOREWORD

———

It is said that the Bible is like an ocean; you can fish deep without touching its depths; you can fish wide without touching its bounds. This was my motivation when amid the COVID pandemic, I set out to do some daily in-depth but down-to-earth reflections with my parishioners and friends on social media. The fruit of what seemed to be a dream is what has brought to birth this book to enhance our encounter with the Lord in the scriptures. In this edition of the series I have dubbed *Like an Ocean*, I set out to reflect on the daily gospel readings for the Lenten and the Easter seasons. My focus is to incarnate the Word of God in the day-to-day life situations of Christ's Faithful. It is also to give some insights to brother priests and seminarians as they reflect to break God's Word in the assembly of the faithful. Though sometimes rather technical and scholarly, I have nevertheless aimed to make God's Word speak to the current realities of our lives as Christians. The preacher never preaches alone, so I have fallen on many known and unknown preachers around the world who have all offered insightful thoughts that have added value to this project. I'm grateful to God whose enlightenment directed my thoughts and meditations, the Blessed Mother, whose intercession gave me the stamina to go on, St. Joseph, whose patronage and intercession sent God's constant providence my way, my parishioners in Plum City and Arkansaw, Wisconsin as well as those at the University of Ghana Catholic Chaplaincy and friends, who gave me the reason to burn the midnight candle to put these reflections together. I owe an equal debt of gratitude to the staff and students of St. Paul's Catholic Major Seminary in Accra whose encouragements and environment gave me the impetus to translate this dream into reality. My prayer is that, even as you journey with me through our daily meditations on Holy Scripture, God will increase you in faith, hope and love. May He prepare all who join us in this faith journey to be renewed and be abundantly blessed in the name of the Trinity.

ASH WEDNESDAY

Matthew 6:1-6, 16-18

Give alms, pray and fast

As we begin Lent today, teach us to fast, Lord. Teach us to govern our urges and instincts, to be the masters of our passions and not their slaves. Teach us to be free to give the gifts of ourselves and our talents totally to you and our neighbors. Teach us to make loving sacrifices as much a part of our lives as it was a part of yours. May our Lenten observance this year be fruitful and meaningful. May it enable us to be united with you in prayer, to see you more clearly, love you more dearly, and follow you more closely day by day.

Thursday After Ash Wednesday

Luke 9:22-25

"If anyone wishes to come after me, he must deny himself and take up his cross daily and follow me."

Jesus Christ came into the world to establish the Kingdom of his Father's glory. His whole life looked as if he aimed at forming a cream of followers who would propagate the Kingdom he came to build. In the early hours of his public ministry, he set for himself the task of calling his disciples to be with him in order to be sent out to proclaim his kingdom and preach repentance. He had the whole world to conquer. So he obviously needed adequate hands, ready and willing to further his kingdom. When his own time on earth was rather brief, one would anticipate some urgency and pampering gentility with which he would coax his disciples to follow him. However, that would not be the case. Far from calling them and giving them the promise that the journey would be easy, Jesus demands of them to take up their crosses daily and follow. No one wants a cross, yet it is the cross that Jesus uses as a means for his call to discipleship.

By this act, Jesus teaches us that Crosses are inevitable and no one can follow him adequately well without accepting to take up his/her cross daily. The good news is that our crosses are meaningful if we carry them with Jesus in the lead. Every true follower of Jesus has a cross to bear. He himself went the way of the Cross so as to blaze the trail and offer himself as an example for us so that taking up our crosses and following him in life and death, we may be made holy and blameless in his sight.

Jesus also underscores his honesty with his followers. When he needed to make disciples to carry on his mission, he never lied to them. Life in him demanded crosses, painful sacrifices and even shameful death; but he minced no words in telling them as it is. He plainly laid the cards on the table to allow his followers to freely make an informed decision to follow him without any coercion.

Jesus carried his Cross, he dealt honestly with his followers. He did so to offer himself as an example for us to imitate. On this Lenten day, may our resolve to carry our crosses daily be heightened and may our honesty with one another take after that of Jesus.

My Jesus, without pout, you carried your cross to Calvary to die for my sins. Through my own sacrifices, sorrows and pains, may I join my cross to yours and follow you in all honesty and sincerity.

FRIDAY AFTER ASH WEDNESDAY

Matthew 9:14-15

"The days will come when the bridegroom is taken away from them, and then they will fast."

What can I fast on today?

Will it supply a genuine need?

Will it serve my spiritual growth?

No one fasts for the sake of it. My fasting is never an end in itself. Like the springboard, it is a means to an end. It has meaning only when it adds value to another person's life. It has meaning only when it brings me to appreciate the plight of those who suffer want and go hungry; only when it allows me to put myself in their shoes and take steps to go to their aid. It has value only because it enhances my spiritual growth and ensures my spiritual welfare. It has value only because it disposes me to deepen my prayer life and strengthens my bond with my God. My fasting is no fasting if does not enable me to give up all that is selfish within me and be generous in sacrificing myself and my time for others in their need.

Saturday After Ash Wednesday

Luke 5:27-32

"Those who are healthy do not need a
physician, but the sick do."

A priest went on a pastoral visit to a very remote village in Ghana. As he made his evening rounds visiting the homes of his flock. He passed by the house of a notorious criminal in town. This man was tipped for any evil that was perpetrated in the village and its environs. Everyone knew him to be cruel. He would rob, maim and kill without qualms and no one dared to challenge him. For the fear that anyone who dared to correct him or bring him to justice would eventually sign his death warrant, the police were helpless at the sight of him. Just as the priest had decided to pass by this man's house without looking his way, a voice cried through the window, accosting the priest and pleading with him to visit his house too. Afraid but yet courageous, the priest heeded his call and entered the house of the village criminal. Whiles with him, Father discovered that he had been badly injured and was in danger of losing his limb. He told Father how he got badly injured in the cause of rescuing a helpless woman who was waylaid by a bunch of robbers. When the robbers couldn't harm the woman, they turned the rage at him, beat him up, shot him in the leg, and left him for dead. Since no one would come to his rescue, he crawled home, and because he was a wanted man in the community, he hid himself in his room and tried to nurse his wound all by himself. Unfortunately, the bullet caused his foot the begin rotting away. It was at this point that he made his stress call to the priest who passed his way. In his long conversation with the priest, he opened up, poured his heart out, and told the priest how much he had always desired to make a return to God and how often people had judged and condemned him and made his desired return to God unattractive and impossible. He expressed his wish to receive the sacrament of reconciliation which he had abandoned for ages. The priest heard his confession and carried him to the nearby hospital where attempts were made to salvage his limb. Unfortunately, it was too late and since not much could be done save his limb, it was completely removed. He looked to be making a good recovery when all of a sudden, he took a turn for the worse and gave the ghost. Then came his funeral. Every soul in the village was waiting to see if the priest would bury such a hardened criminal. When to their displeasure the priest organized a fitting burial for his repentant friend, the whole community turned their heels against the priest- he had committed an abomination. He did not only enter the house of the notorious criminal, but he also brought him to God's house to give him a befitting burial. It was when the people kept pestering the priest for his kindness to the one the whole world had condemned that he quoted them the proverb, "Those who are healthy do not need a physician, but the sick do." For this priest, and all who believe in Jesus as the face of God's mercy, the steadfast love of the Lord never ceases. His mercies never come to an end. God is faithful even when we are not. His wish is not for the death of the evil person but for the evil person to turn away from sin and live.

God is love. His love embraces the sinner and makes him whole. May he wrap his mantle around me in this season of grace, cleanse me of my sin and make me a means of his love and mercy.

First Sunday Of Lent

"At that time Jesus was led by the Spirit into
the desert to be tempted by the devil."

Lent is Here Again

Dear friends in Christ, all too soon, Lent is here with us again. In the middle of the past week, we celebrated Ash Wednesday to mark the beginning of the Lenten season. We were all signed with ashes to remind us that we are dust and to dust, we shall return.

The ashes marked a call on us to repent and believe in the gospel. They communicated other eternal truths that should not be easily dismissed.

Firstly the ashes told us that we are sinners. Much as we remain God's children and so belong to God, we are still children of this fallen world. Ashes are lifeless dust. Insofar as we still give in to our tendencies, to selfishness and sin, we are as lifeless as dust. Sin separates us from God, who is the source of all life. Without God's redeeming spirit in us, we would have no hope of eternal life.

Secondly, the ashes reminded us that our sins and acts of selfishness, cause damage. On the past Palm Sunday, we all carried palm branches to mark the victory of Christ over sin. These were the branches from which the ashes were made. The truth needs to be told that our sins dent and forfeit that victory. Just as the palm branches with which we joyfully sang hosanna to the King were destroyed to make the ashes, so does sin destroy our life of grace in God.

Thirdly, the ashes reminded us that despite our sins and our deep-seated selfishness, God has not given up on us. Christ our Redeemer claims us for his own. We still have a mission in his Kingdom. Christ still wants us to be His ambassadors. We were marked with ashes because we are sinners. However, the mark was given in the sign of Christ's cross, which won for us the grace of a fresh start and a new life.

We were marked on our foreheads because ours is the mission to go boldly into the world as Christ's representatives. Christ wants to change the world through us. The ashes are Christ's way of inviting us to make a fresh start. Lent, therefore, is a season that calls us to a new beginning.

Dear friends, there is a tendency every year for many to treat this all-important season like one of the ordinary routines in the church's life. For some of us, life goes on as it was in the beginning. One can thus hardly tell the difference for such people. They hate, quarrel, eat, drink, play, make merry, and go about their businesses, fair or foul, with little or no thought of the golden opportunity for a fresh start. Some others see Lent as a relic that has fallen into disuse, a primitive torture device that our world has outgrown.

Yet many others see Lent as a depressing time of penance, a time of insipid mortification, a necessary evil that must be stoically lived and dropped. They mechanically reduce their diet, half-heartedly try some kindness, with reluctance augment their initial resolve to intensify their prayer lives and count down to Easter only to forget this season of grace with a sigh of relief for another year.

Nevertheless, Lent is a time for us to open fresh pages in our lives. A time to commit ourselves to doing ordinary good things extraordinarily well. Perhaps we may give up eating between meals, sweets, smoking, or drinking. We could begin attending Mass more frequently than we have done in the past or frequent the Sacrament of Penance. Maybe we would want to pray more and decide to keep God constantly present in our consciousness. Reading a spiritual book to boost our faith could do for some people. Many others could give themselves to practicing some corporal works of Mercy such as visiting the sick and the aged. The important thing here is to do these with the right disposition and a Christian motive.

Lent is also a time of renewal. It is a time we renew our baptism. We die with Christ to rise with him. Such a death is realized only through our baptism. By our baptism, we are buried with Christ unto death, so that by his rising from the dead to the glory of the Father, we may also walk in the newness of life (Rom. 6:3). In the time of Noah, when sin took over every fiber of society, God cleansed the world by the waters of the flood. This event, alluded to in this Sunday liturgy has baptismal undertones. In the new dispensation, Jesus hallowed the waters of baptism by availing himself for John to baptize him to fulfill all righteousness. By plunging into the waters of baptism, Christ died to sin once and for all. In our own baptism, we die with him to the self and to sin. Death of this nature is what Lent brings to focus as we make this forty-day journey through the wilderness of life. Lent for us then must be dying to the self. Death to self involves metanoia, a conversion, a turning away from self-centeredness. It in effect involves interior conversion.

Interior repentance is a radical reorientation of our whole life, a return, a conversion to God with all our heart, an end of sin, a turning away from evil, with repugnance toward the evil actions we have committed. At the same time, it entails the desire and resolution to change one's life, with hope in God's mercy and trust in the help of his grace. This conversion of heart is accompanied by a salutary pain and sadness which the Church Fathers called *animi cruciatus*- an affliction of spirit and *compunctio cordis* -repentance of heart (see CCC. 1431).

This turn away from the self must necessarily lead to a turn toward God and neighbor. This is why Lent is a season that also invites us to transform our attitude towards God in the first place and also our attitude towards our neighbor. Lent, therefore, calls on us to obey the supreme command of love. Loving God anew with all our bodies, with all our hearts, and with all our souls. It also invites us to change our hearts toward our neighbor, family, community, parish, and society at large. There is thus a communal dimension to Lent. It is for this reason that in this season the Church prays imploring God not only to release us from the chains of sin but also to protect us from all adversity. It doesn't take time for one to spot the all-inclusive language the Church uses during Lent. Suffice to say that the call to love is as necessary as the call to conversion. Conversion is a turning away from self-centeredness and substituting that with the love of God and neighbor. Our fasting, prayer, and alms-giving will be meaningless if our love of God and neighbor does not remain the active driving force in our daily endeavors. Our goal in Lent, therefore, is to increase our love for God in Himself and our love for Him in our neighbor. As E. A. Lawrence once put it, "when the Lent of life is over, love alone will remain."

Dear friends, in this season, we may take ashes, we may open fresh pages in our lives, we may relive our baptismal experience of death to sin and life in Christ, we may embrace a sincere change of heart and a heightened sense of love for God and neighbor, nonetheless, we must be encouraged by the fact that all our Lenten observances are meant to restrain our faults, raise up our minds, hearts, and wills to God, and bestow both virtue and its rewards on us through Christ our Lord. There is thus everything in this season for us to gain. Let us then brace ourselves and actively live every moment of it in spirit and truth.

As we do on every First Sunday of Lent, we reflect today on Jesus' temptation in the desert. The truth is that, when Jesus was tempted, he had just been baptized; he had just been led by the Spirit; he had fasted for 40 days and was hungry and weak; he was alone amidst the harshest desert weather conditions.

My Jesus, I don't know when, where, and how my own temptations might come, but when they do, please be my security as you enable me to find consolation and escape in your Word.

Monday Of The First Week Of Lent

Matthew 25:21-46

'Amen, I say to you, whatever you did for one of
these least brothers of mine, you did for me.'

Both goats and sheep saw the hungry, the stranger, the naked, the sick, and the imprisoned.

Whereas the goats saw the least among men, only as good as to be ignored, to be shunned, and to be put down, the sheep saw brothers and sisters as good enough to be loved and to be catered for. In the end, the sheep rendered service, not to men but to Christ.

My Jesus, Open my eyes today to see you in the less fortunate and incline my heart and will to render them pure and selfless service. Make of me that good and faithful servant who is deserving of the kingdom prepared for the righteous from the foundation of the world.

Tuesday Of The First Week Of Lent

Mark 6:7-15

"Your Father knows what you need before you ask him."

Jesus told his disciples not to babble at prayer. He then taught them the "Our Father".

He seemed to suggest that the key to effective prayer is simplicity. That which is simple is devoid of duplicity. That which is simple has no guile in it. Inherent in it is honesty, frankness, and a display of innocence and trust.

In its simplicity, prayer never attempts at tricking God or coercing him to do our bidding. It rather demonstrates our trust in God's dependability and our readiness to count on him despite ourselves.

There's nothing more consoling than going to prayer knowing that he knows it even before we ask.

When we keep it simple and concise, prayer pierces the clouds, touches the skies, and changes things. It transforms the totality of our being and grows our intimacy with God, whom we dare to call Abba.

Let us be diligent in prayer and let our prayers be perseveringly lacking of all guile and duplicity. A sincere three-worded prayer, uttered in faith and secret might accomplish more than a bunch of empty words uttered publicly to win people's admiration. We cannot twist his arm to do our will. He knows and loves us more than we do ourselves.

Lord Jesus Christ, Son of God, have mercy on me, a sinner.

WEDNESDAY OF THE FIRST WEEK OF LENT

LUKE 11:29-32

"At the judgment, the men of Nineveh will arise with this generation and condemn it, because at the preaching of Jonah they repented, and there is something greater than Jonah here."

Jesus came that we may have life and have it to the full. The wages of sin is death.

If anything deprives me of life, it is sin. Jesus, therefore, came that I may eschew sin and have life in abundance. Such was the mission of Jonah. He was sent that the people of Nineveh might turn away from sin and live. Fortunately, the Ninevites listened, believed, and acted on Jonah's word.

If despite the limitations in his person as a prophet, the people of Nineveh still heeded Jonah's message and turned from sin, how much more should I and my generation heed the promptings of the Son of God who came to conquer sin and give us life to the full!

Today, Jesus comes to me every day in the power of his Word. He makes an entrance into my life in his body and blood, soul, and divinity. I disappoint him when his presence in Word and sacrament does not renew my commitment to fight and conquer the sin in me and embrace the life he brings in abundance.

My Jesus, pardon my sin, grant me the grace to run away from sin and live to the full by the promptings of your word and the power of your sacrament.

Thursday Of The First Week Of Lent

Matthew 7:7-11

"Ask and it will be given to you; seek and you will
find; knock and the door will be opened to you."

Sometimes, the journey of life is like pulling carts loaded with the stones of doubts, failures, disappointments, sufferings, frustrations, and hardships. If we become men and women of prayer, we will not only find the strength to keep on pulling but also realize that the Holy Spirit, the master architect, will build those stones of suffering into beautiful spiritual edifices, glorifying God and filling our hearts with joy for all eternity.

My Jesus, when I am weak and heavy laden; when I am cambered with loads of cares, may you alone be my refuge. May I never tire to take everything to you in prayer and when I do, may your mercy and kindness enable me to find solace in you.

Friday Of The First Week Of Lent

Matthew 5:20-26

"But I say to you, whoever is angry with his
brother will be liable to judgment."

God is slow to anger and rich in mercy. We who are made in his image
must reflect him. When anger moves us to burn bridges, hurl insults and
feed resentments we contradict God's image and likeness in us. May the
spirit of forgiveness and reconciliation enable us to reflect that image of
God that we are meant to be.

My Jesus, when the might of my pain and hurt hardens my heart and
truncates my capacity to forgive, may your example from the Cross grant
me the impetus to let go and let God.

SATURDAY OF THE FIRST WEEK OF LENT

Matthew 5:43-48

"You have heard it said you shall love your neighbor
and hate your enemies, but I say to you: love your
enemies and pray for your persecutors."

Lent is a time we strive to be righteous. Righteousness, as the term depicts, is about being right. It is about being right in one's relationships. Its three dimensions find fulfillment in the right relationship with God, with neighbor, and with the totality of God's creation. The righteous person is thus the one who is at rights in his/ her relationship with God, neighbor, and creation. Today's reading draws our attention to our relationship with our neighbor. For the Israelites, a neighbor is simply the one who dwells next to me. He dwells next to me because he is on good terms with me. He dwells next to me because he sees life the way I do and dances to the same tunes I dance to. Such a person is either a fellow Jew or a stranger whose worldview is not offensive to me. Love of neighbor then was simply understood as love which binds me and my family, me and my friends, me and my companions. Hardly would love encompass an enemy or a persecutor. When Jesus turned the tables and demanded of his disciples, true Love for their enemies, he introduced a new and radical law. Nowhere does the radical newness of the Christian ethic stand out more clearly than in Christ's simple phrase: "Love your enemies and pray for your persecutors." Jesus calls his followers to that unconquerable love which loves without counting who or what a person is nor what a person might have done to offend me. He invites his followers to that indiscriminate love which knows no bitterness or vindictiveness towards anybody whatsoever. We might have every good reason to pay another in their own coin, yet love in Christ sets no boundaries in our right relationship with any human person. Love demands of us to beat our swords into plowshares and our spears into pruning hooks. Like the sun of God which shines on both the good and the evil, our love must indiscriminately shine forth on friend and foe alike.

Today, may we strive to expand the boundaries of our love. May we seek to uproot all bitterness, bury our rancors, and bridge our socio-political differences. May our love for all be genuine, sincere, and impartial. May we love because we love.

My God, we were yet sinners when your love sent forth your Son to die to make us your children again. In him, you showed us how much you loved us even when sin made us your enemies. Teach me to love just as you do.

Second Sunday Of Lent

"Jesus took Peter, James, and John his brother, and
led them up a high mountain by themselves."

The Transfiguration offers us the opportunity to reflect on the pillars of
Lent. In the Lenten season, the Church bids us fast, pray and give alms.

At the foot of the mountain is the Fertile Crescent, a sign of abundance,
a representation of the fruits of the earth and the works of human hands.
He who leaves the Fertile Crescent in effect leaves behind his daily bread;
leaves behind material joys and abstains from all that physically sustains
the body. Thus climbing the mount of transfiguration, Jesus and his trio
did fast and abstain.

A mountain top is a place of encounter with God. Whoever climbs the
mountain does so in order to pray. Not only did the group hear God
speak to them, but they also experienced the richness of the Law and the
Prophet. They made an encounter with God and his word- something
prayer does for us.

Then they wouldn't build tents up there to perpetuate the rich experience
they made up the mountain. They had to come down to translate their
experience into the lives of the people at the foot of the mountain.

Today we are encouraged not to be afraid but to rise up and make an ascent
to the mountain denying ourselves of things we cherish for the sake of
God. We are encouraged to take a leaf out of our schedules to commune
with God in prayer, and as our fasting and prayer grow us in holiness,

may our taste of sanctity enable us to reach out in kindness to the poor and the needy.

My Jesus, may I resolve to deny myself of something dear and grow intimate with you in prayer even as you grant me the grace of charity to make a difference in other people's lives.

Monday Of The Second Week Of Lent

Luke 6:36-38

"Be merciful, just as your Father is merciful."

Whenever I think of mercy, I also think of compassion. It is as if these two words go together. To be merciful is to be compassionate. The early Romans used the term misericordia to describe merciful. Miser and Cordia are two interesting words. It is from miser that we derive the English misery. To be in misery is to be distraught, it is to be broken into pieces. Cordia has to do with the heart. The merciful person is the one who allows his heart to be broken for the sake of another's mistake or mishap. While we were still sinners, God broke his heart and sent his Son to die for us. He put himself in a state of discomfort, just so that we will be relieved from our state of wretchedness.

Compassion is from the Latin, cum, and patire. It literally means to suffer with, to feel with. For some people, it means to bear with. When we carry the pain and the troubles of others with them, what we do is to make their burden easy to bear, what we do is to suffer with them the pain they bear even when they are the ones who brought it upon themselves. Compassion makes me treat the other person as a subject and not as an object. In compassion, I am able to put myself in the shoes of the other and feel his or her pinch and treat them with kindness and gentleness.

Today, we are called to be as merciful as our Heavenly Father is merciful.

God's heart breaks always on our account. He bears the pain and burden of our shortcomings without judging or condemning us. It is up to us to do the same with one another. It is very easy to judge and condemned another even when the given limitations are obvious in us. Yet ours is the call to treat one another as we would want God to treat us when we falter.

My Jesus, grant me the serenity to let my heartbreak at the fault of others and help them to bear the burden of their limitations. Whenever I am tempted to judge and condemn others, open my eyes to my own limitations and grant me the spirit of empathy to tolerate them and give them as many chances as you give me every day.

TUESDAY OF THE SECOND WEEK OF LENT

Matthew 23:1-12

"Whoever exalts himself will be humbled, but whoever humbles himself will be exalted."

The Latin terms minister, ministris translate as a servant. They have everything to do with service. It is from these that a distinction is made between the ministerial priesthood and common priesthood. The ministerial priest is the servant priest. His priestly office is exercised in service. His desire is not to lord it over the flock and satisfy his selfish wants but to lay down his life in selfless service to them. He eschews pride and taking after his Lord, who did not count equality with God something to grasp, acts in humility in the interest of God's people. Like the ministerial priest, every Christian is called to a life of service. However, there is the temptation for the Christian to take his position and use it for comfort, for power, for prestige; and for self-indulgence. Times are when we pervert our faith and claim to be busily doing greater things for God which in effect are selfish and self-serving. In our self-service ventures, the ego takes the center stage, making us the zenith of the universe and masters of all we survey. That we will not be led astray by pride and its attendant accolades, but be driven by the spirit of humble service, Jesus challenges us today and calls us to a life of humility. He encourages us not to follow the bad examples of the religious elites of his day. They had allowed their pride to lead the way. In the process, they lost that which really mattered. As we go through this day of Lent, let us resolve to conduct our affairs in all humble service to God and neighbor, forgetting the self and putting others first.

My Jesus, pride they say goes before the fall, grant me the grace to spot it when it rears its ugly head, so that I may follow you in humility and simplicity as I serve you in others.

WEDNESDAY OF THE SECOND WEEK OF LENT

Matthew 20:17-28

"Whoever wishes to be first among you shall be your slave."

Jesus, en route to Jerusalem, predicted his impending passion and death. James and John saw it as an opportunity to seize their chances. Through their mother, they sought places of prominence in Jesus' kingdom. They showed no sympathy for Jesus' plight nor care for the sensibilities of the other disciples. They selfishly sought for what was in it for them. Obviously, their individualism incurred the displeasure of the others who became indignant upon hearing of their attempt at usurping places of honor in Jesus' kingdom. Jesus saw this as an occasion for catechesis. He distinguished between authority among the Gentiles and authority among his own. In the former, authority ought to be imposed and felt. In the latter, authority is service and is altruistic. In Jesus' own words, "You know that the rulers of the Gentiles lord it over them, and the great ones make their authority over them felt. But it shall not be so among you. Rather, whoever wishes to be great among you shall be your servant; whoever wishes to be first among you shall be your slave."

In 2019, the world rose to a spectacular phenomenon when in a 10km athletic competition, Simon Cheprot helped a fallen colleague Kinrono Kilkendi cross the finishing line and lost his place as the top contender in the process. Simon helped a colleague who nearly collapsed. When he had to choose between fame and friendship, he chose to help a friend in need.

He and his colleague came last in the competition and yet he is known today for the service he rendered and the duo are shining ambassadors of peace, unity, and friendship. None of the athletes who placed first in the competition is remembered as well as Simon. Stopping to serve the need of his fallen colleague, he placed last in the tournament. Yet, he is remembered more for his service than for his position in the tournament.

Many a time, in our bid to win the race of life, we care less about and grow insensitive to the needs of others. We forgo our call to humble service and focus on our selfish interests to the neglect of the service of Christian charity we owe one another. Just as the Son of Man came not to be served but to serve and to give his life as a ransom for many, so are we called to empty ourselves of all pride and fix our gaze on the needs of others.

My Jesus, when my sinful pride robs me of the spirit of humble service to others, may your grace ginger in me the spirit that moved you to serve instead of being served.

THURSDAY OF THE SECOND
WEEK OF LENT

Luke 16:19-31

"...lying at his door was a poor man named Lazarus,
covered with sores, who would gladly have eaten his fill
of the scraps that fell from the rich man's table."

Jesus is great when he teaches in stories. His story about the Rich-man
and Lazarus is a masterpiece. Every detail of it is quite revealing. The
rich man we are told, dresses in purple and linen and dines sumptuously
daily- Purple for his royalty, linen for his priestly character and sumptuous
dining for affluence. Per his outfit, he professes that there is nothing he has
and nothing he consumes which he never received. Royalty comes with
great inheritance whiles the priesthood attracts mass social beneficence
and assistance. If he is rich, it is because his palm kernel has been cracked
for him by a benevolent spirit. The last thing such a person would forget
is kindness to a neighbor.

The word Neighbor is from neigh= near or next and ghebor = dwell. My
neighbor is the one who dwells near or next to me. Jesus in this parable says
that Lazarus dwelt at the gate of the rich man. Thus, he was a neighbor
to the rich man. They had nothing in common. One was poor, the other
was rich but because Lazarus dwelt near the rich man, the rich man whose
palm kernel had been cracked by benevolence ought to have been kind
enough to nourish and cherish him. In fact, he didn't have to do so much

to cater to Lazarus. He only needed just a little effort as Lazarus would have gladly welcomed table scraps.

So today we are called to remember first and foremost that there is nothing we have which we did not receive. Even what we work for, we receive. We are therefore, stewards of our goods and properties. Secondly, that we owe a neighbor a duty of kindness which we must not neglect.

The neighbor must not necessarily be a friend or a relative. He could be a total stranger or even an enemy, yet we must nourish and cherish. We should put in the least effort we can to lavish them with charity without measure.

Whenever I sat by someone on the train, on the bus, or on the plane in total neglect, whenever I failed to see a person in need as my opportunity to be a neighbor, whenever I neglected the marginalized and failed to speak for the speechless, whenever I looked away when I could have lifted a finger to help the helpless, I'm that purple-linen clad rich man who professed to be a steward of God and yet refused to employ God's gifts for the benefit of a needy neighbor.

My Jesus, giver of all that is good, create in me that positional consciousness that will enable me to open my eyes to the plight of others and the courage not to sit aloof but to lift a finger to offer them relief for the glory of your name.

FRIDAY OF THE SECOND WEEK OF LENT

Matthew 21:33-43, 45-46

"The stone that the builders rejected has become
the cornerstone; by the Lord has this been
done, and it is wonderful in our eyes? "

The philosophy of individualism has permeated every facet of our social structure. Nowadays, people are given to promoting the exercise of an individual's own goals and desires with very little consideration for objective values. Bring an individual or a group of individuals to a given project and the first thing they look for is "what is in it for me?" For instance, people enter into politics and other professions, and their driving motive is what they can individually gain in the final analysis. Almost six out of every ten people we meet today have the tendency of advancing their individual interests to the detriment of other people's interests or the common good. As individualism progresses, people have no qualms hating others they consider as threats to their personal interests. It is commonplace for people to malign each other all to further individual personal ambitions. Many others care even less if they have to kill to satisfy their whims and caprices. The worse of it is when we allow individualism to rear its head in our dealings with God. Today, people are ready to shelve or kill God, just so they can have their way.

The parable of the wicked tenants is another of Jesus' masterpieces which invites us to be wary of individualism. Here, the landowner planted his vineyard and entrusted it to tenants who had to manage it and deliver his due at harvest. Unfortunately, when the harvest was due, the tenants, having been characterized by the possessive spirit of individualism, concerned themselves more with what was in it for them, rather than what was in it for the owner. In the process, they forgot themselves as mere managers and mistreated the owner's servants and even killed some. In patience, he sent in more servants but to no avail. Thinking they might respect his son he took a chance and sent his own son but him also they killed. Jesus' hearers supposed that the master would kill these wicked, selfish and individualistic tenants. However, Jesus' reaction is quite intriguing: "Did you never read in the Scriptures:

The stone that the builders rejected has become the cornerstone; by the Lord has this been done, and it is wonderful in our eyes? "

Here, Jesus seems to be saying that far from killing the wicked tenants, the Landowner would not act in accordance with their conduct. Rather, the son whom they rejected and killed would be the cornerstone that would hold the spiritual household of the wicked tenants together. Thus, in spite of the rejection and the execution of his son, the landowner would still be patient enough to transform their wickedness into a means of salvation. This is the picture of God Jesus paints.

In our selfishness, we can hurt God but God does not pay us in our own coin. We might reject and execute even his Son but the stone we reject, God will marvelously set up as a cornerstone to hold the edifice of our faith together.

Today, let's all be reminded of the dangers of individualism. It can lead us to lose our sense of appreciation, it can make us hate and kill even God. It can blind us to the good that God graciously lavishes on us.

Let us also remember that our God is patient with us. Time and again he gives us another chance; and even when our conduct calls for his displeasure, he does not mark our guilt and deal with us according to our faults, rather, he makes things work for our good. Ours is to see his patience as an opportunity to be saved. If we blow all the chances he offers we might compel him to allow us to know decay at the end of time.

My Jesus, when my selfishness pushes me to take you for granted, may your none retaliatory spirit afford me another chance as your grace enables me to grow in choosing your will over my myopic interests.

SATURDAY OF THE SECOND WEEK OF LENT

LUKE 15:11-32

"Your brother has returned and your father has slaughtered the fattened calf because he has him back safe and sound."

The tongue, they say, has no bone but it can break a heart. Whenever I read the story of the prodigal son, my heart jumps on account of the servant who broke the news of the ongoing party to the elder brother. The details of his brief exposé to the elder brother were good enough to ginger envy, jealousy, and anger; and if that is what he intended, he achieved exactly that. My question is: Did he have to spell out the details the way he did? Could he not have simply told the elder brother of the younger brother's return which had necessitated a celebration? No wonder the elder brother would reference his father for not giving him even a kid to celebrate with his friends. What did this servant do? He only fanned the elder brother's anger into flames. He transformed into a source of bitterness an occasion which should have brought joy to an entire household. He succeeded in keeping out a son who should have naturally joined in the celebration of the return of an erring brother. He robbed the elder brother of the foretaste of what goes on in heaven. He had no clue of the real meaning of the father's action. He had no share in the father's mercy- he distanced himself from it and set the stage for envy and jealousy. He himself had an issue with his master's kindness toward his prodigal son and succeeded in roping the elder brother into his bitterness. If he had but used his tongue wisely and his words judiciously, perhaps he would have helped the elder brother to appreciate his father's love and mercy towards his own brother.

If all of us would learn to use our tongues wisely, and calculate our words in all our discourses, we would make our world a better place to live. It is better not to speak unless what we say is more golden than silence.

My Jesus, help me to keep this my big mouth shut until I know what I am talking about and have weighed its impact on people and situations.

Monday Of The Third Week Of Lent

Luke 4:24-30

"But he passed through the midst of them and went away."

Jesus finds no hospitality in his hometown. His people know him too well to accept his credentials as the Messiah. The carpenter's son, Mary's boy can never be The One who is to come. He can not even be a prophet.

Familiarity, they say, breeds disrespect. We commonly only get enraged at people we respect less. Take time to examine the people we normally get mad at and pour contempt on. They are usually people we know too well to easily disrespect- our husbands, wives, children, coworkers or subordinates, people we have grown very used to. Had the people of Nazareth got some respect for Jesus, they would have even smiled at an insult from him. However, because they held him in low esteem, if not in contempt, and because they never deemed him fit for their kindest regard, not only were they angry at him, they even dared to drive him to the outskirts of their town, to the brow of the hill their village was situated, to hurl him down. Yet, Truth can never be toppled and the life of the Son of God can not be taken until he himself decides to lay it down. So despite their effort to throw him down, he only passed through their midst and walked away.

Our world could decide to treat our God with contempt. They could even feign to know him too well as to treat him with spite, they might take calculating steps to subtract him from public spaces and smear his image in the mud. All the same, he is all in all. He is True God from True God.

He is the Way, the Truth, and the Life. His Kingdom shall prevail and his truth shall forever stand.

My Jesus, when the world deems you to be too simplistic a person for a Messiah, grant me the grace to find in you a Saviour who alone can transform the helplessness and hopelessness of my life into a meaningful venture.

TUESDAY OF THE THIRD WEEK OF LENT

Matthew 18:21-35

Jesus answered, "I say to you, not seven
times but seventy-seven times."

Unforgiveness, it is said, is like drinking the poisonous potion and expecting the other person to die.

If there is a virus that kills the human person slowly but surely, it is our resolve not to let go and forgive. Through lack of forgiveness, many a man walks the face of the earth half dead; and many more have died prematurely as a result of the venoms they self imbibed on account of their inability to forgive a past wrong.

It is thus not surprising that when Peter had the chance to seek direction from the Lord as to the extent one could go regarding forgiveness, he decided to do what no man could do. "Lord, if my brother sins against me, how often must I forgive him? As many as seven times?"

In his mind, Peter had been very thorough and perfectly generous in proposing sevenfold forgiveness. This is because to the Jew, seven is a perfect number and to have forgiven seven times is to have done a perfect act of kindness. Seven is also the sum of 3 and 4. Whereas 3 symbolizes divinity, 4 symbolizes the ends of the earth. 7 is, therefore, a union of the divine and the universe. The only one who has the ability to unite heaven and earth is God. He alone has the power to reconcile himself to the earth and that is what he did in the incarnation. When the Word was made flesh and dwelt among us, heaven was wedded to the earth and man and God were reconciled. To unite 3 and 4 in the act of forgiveness was for Peter to forgive the way only God could. After all the prophet Amos opines that God forgives only for three transgressions and for four and does not revoke the punishment.

It was therefore surprising that Jesus demanded rather a seventy, seven times forgiveness. Jesus knows how unforgiveness can destroy us in mind and in body. He also knows that as long as we live with one another we shall hurt and be hurt and the only way to gain our sanity is to forgive and be forgiven.

Incidentally, there is a tendency for us to seek justice in the face of our hurts. Erroneously, we believe that the peace we forfeit on account of unforgiveness will only be restored by justice. We, therefore, in the face of our hurts, look forward to certain milestones of justice: arrests, trials, guilty sentences and the execution of the culprit. However, justice never really brings us peace. The truth is that it is only when we are able to forgive that we are also able to overcome the anger, the hate, the pain and the shame that go with the hurt. When I choose to forgive is when I liberate myself from the self-imposed imprisonment my lack of forgiveness brings.

When Jesus made the seventy times seven demand for forgiveness therefore, all he did was to keep us alive and to save us from unduly imprisoning ourselves. His quantum of times we need to forgive drives home the fact that forgiveness is not an occasional act but rather a permanent attitude (cf M.L. King). Every occasion we have to catch a breath is an equal occasion to forgive an erring brother or sister. The ball is in our court.

My Jesus, help me to constantly guard my relationships. In the face of fallouts, may I never hesitate to seek reconciliation. May the spirit of forgiveness permeate every facet of my life so that I will forgive others just as you forgive my excesses.

WEDNESDAY OF THE THIRD WEEK OF LENT

Matthew 5:17-19

"Amen, I say to you, until heaven and earth pass away, not the smallest letter or the smallest part of a letter will pass from the law until all things have taken place."

Love, they say, never ends.

In his discourse on the Law, Jesus made it crystal clear that he had come not to destroy but to fulfill the law. He assured his listeners that even if heaven and earth should pass away, not an iota of the law would pass away. Elsewhere, summing up the law, he said that the epitome of the law is in the love of God and love of neighbor. For Jesus therefore, love is either coterminous with the law or it is the fullness of the law. St. John the evangelist affirmed it when he opined that to love is to obey the commandment of God (see 1 Jn 5:3). For Jesus to say therefore that he had come not to abolish the law is tantamount to saying he had come not to destroy the law of love but fulfill it. He himself came into the world because God so loved the world. If no iota of the law will pass away, then no amount of love should pass away even with the passage of heaven and earth. Love, therefore, is as eternal as the law of God. Our call to obey the law then is a call to love God with all our hearts, all our minds and with all our bodies and to love our neighbor as ourselves.

To obey the law and to teach others to do the same is to love and encourage love in others. To do otherwise is to hate and attract others to do the same.

The question is: How much love do I find in my heart? How much love have I encouraged in others? Do I create a conducive environment for others to love or I set the stage for them to hate and be bitter? Do I sow seeds of discord or I build a fraternity of peace, love, and harmony? Today, if Jesus should do a continuous assessment with me on love and obedience to God's law, will I be counted the greatest or the least in the Kingdom of God?

My Jesus, you made me for love. When life's vicissitudes move my heart to hatred and disobedience to your will, may your grace abound to transform my brokenness and turn me into an instrument of your own love.

THURSDAY OF THE THIRD WEEK OF LENT

Luke 11:14-23

Some of them said, "By the power of Beelzebul,
the prince of demons, he drives out demons."

If we have nothing good to say about someone, let's not say it. I am imagining how different our world would be if we all resolved to say no evil of another person or peddle untruths about others just to defame them. Calumny, slander, and detraction are still sinful, yet they remain the easiest things our world could find in today's average society. Turn on the radio or the TV, skim through the print media and it will take you no time to see how much presenters as well as panelists, columnists as well as reporters are given to skewing the truth and putting others down, casting smears on them, just for selfish gains. Listen to many a political discourse and it will take you no time at all to see how political opponents throw one another under the bus just to win cheap political gains. The story is no different in the arena of faith. Many faith communities have been destroyed because members resorted to slander and calumny to settle scores. Many innocent persons have in recent times been slandered and have had defamatory things said about them which only dented their reputation. Innocent people have lost jobs and positions in life because others detracted them. Some people never climbed the ladder at their workplaces because other colleagues pulled them down with slanders. Perhaps we ourselves have been victims of calumny before and our stars were once dimmed because of some false accusation or an untruth someone else said about us. Not to worry at all. Jesus was there too. Today he exorcises a mute man. When the demon had left the man, some onlookers said he acted in the power of Beelzebul. Others demanded of him a sign to test him. All they meant to do was to detract Jesus. Without warring with them, Jesus took time to point it out to them that if Satan should fight Satan, his divided kingdom would fall. He further pointed to the power with which their own people drove out demons and used it as evidence against them. He then told them the essence of his action, saying, "...if it is by the finger of God that I drive out demons, then the Kingdom of God has come upon you."

It is least surprising that Jesus was calumniated when he had exorcised a person. This points to Satan as the source of calumny. Pope Francis states with no uncertain terms that Calumny is worse than sin and it is the direct expression of Satan. Though a sin, calumny, per the Pope's thoughts, is something more. It is born out of everything evil. It originates in hatred and hate is the work of Satan. According to the Holy Father, "Calumny destroys the work of God in people, in their souls." No wonder in our passage, the people attributed the power of God at work in Jesus to the power of Satan, thereby, destroying God's work as manifested in His Son. "Calumny uses lies to get ahead." "Be in no doubt," the Pope said: "Where there is calumny, there is Satan himself."

Friends, one of the easiest temptations we can fall prey to is to make others look awful so we look good. It is very easy for us all to sin by slandering another to further our own course. Perhaps it feels good to be ahead in our carriers but it is devilish if we would want to do so with calumny. The end never justifies the means and no matter what we aim to achieve in the end, others have the right to their reputation and we have the obligation not to sell our souls to the devil by allowing ourselves to be employed as his agents. This is why we are going to resolve to say nothing of another if what we say will bring their image into disrepute. We have been called to fight our life's battles with weapons other than calumny and detraction. Our call is to war with love and forgiveness, praying for our detractors and allowing our silence to speak more loudly to them than falling prey to the evil of calumny.

Lord, may I never gossip today or say any untruth about another. May no thought or action of mine punch a hole in another person's image. Help me to be silent when my speech will only serve to destroy another.

FRIDAY OF THE THIRD WEEK OF LENT

Mark 12:28-34

"Which is the first of all the commandments?"

When God so loved the world, he sent his only begotten son. When Jesus become one like us in all things but sin, he mounted the cross and died to save us. Scripture has it that greater love no man has than to lay down one's life for one's friends. Christ's incarnation and his death on the cross constitute a big event of love. His cross is, therefore, a symbol of love. Its vertical beam points to love which transcends to the heavens and its horizontal beam is a reminder of love as it immanently transpires among us. The totality of the cross speaks to the fact that our love for the divine and that of our neighbor are inseparable. Like the Siamese twins, they go together.

A story is told of a boy 9 and his brother 12. They hailed from a broken home and had an absentee father. As their poor family couldn't make ends meet, they offered to do light jobs to earn a living. They knocked at people's doors and asked for chores to do and errands to run. Sometimes they offered themselves as porters. One day someone asked them to carry her pieces of luggage to the bus terminal. When they got there, the lady gave them a five Ghana Cedi note (say $ 1 bill) which the elder brother received. As soon as the money went to the elder brother, the younger brother got vexed. He began crying uncontrollably to demand his share immediately. Nothing would stop him from crying and no one could convince him to wait till his brother could find him a change. Thinking that if the money was handed to him for keeps till change could come would help, people around asked the elder brother to hand it to him. As soon as he got it, to the surprise of all, he wiped his tears, smiled and tore the money into two halves and gave one half to his brother. You can imagine the hysteria he caused. The atmosphere was charged with so much laughter that none could control themselves.

Why did the people laugh? They laughed because tearing legal tender into two halves doesn't really give it purchasing power. One cannot do any business with one half of any legal tender.

Today, a Scribe asks to know which is the first of the commandments. Jesus' answer? "The first is this: Hear, O Israel! The Lord our God is Lord alone! You shall love the Lord your God with all your heart, with all your soul, with all your mind, and with all your strength. The second is this: You shall love your neighbor as yourself. "

The scribe asked for the first, why did Jesus add the second? Like a legal tender, one cannot tear love into two and expect to live meaningfully on one half. Transcendental love and Immanent love go hand in hand. Saint John the Evangelist says that if a man claims to love God but hates his brother, he is a liar and the truth is not in him. Our love for God only finds fulfillment in our love for neighbor. In much the same way if I have love for a neighbor but no love for God, I am only a philanthropist. Just as the cross has a vertical beam and a horizontal beam, love has transcendence and immanence and he who observes them both dwells in God and God in him.

Today, we are called to carry the cross of love. Ours is to renew our love for God by all standards. How much time do I have for God? How often do I stay connected with him in prayer? Do I lean on him? Do I take all of my strength from him? Do I look up to him? Do I meditate on his word and keep it? Jesus said it, that, if you love me you will keep my word, my father will love you and we shall come to you.

Our love for God should spur in our love for neighbor. Perhaps there is this person I have hard feelings toward. Perhaps there is this grudge I have nurtured for years. Perhaps there is this coworker I have vowed not to have anything to do with. Perhaps my spouse has been such a pain in the neck that I have divorced him completely from my heart. In our world of broken promises and fragile peace, love sometimes becomes a chore too heavy to endure. Today, may Jesus deem us very close to the kingdom not because we know all the right answers to the law of love but because we live the law of love in its transcendence and its immanence every day of our lives.

My Jesus, love brought you into the world and love made you mount the cross. Just as by love's promptings you obeyed the will of the father and also laid down your life for me, may your spirit inspire in me love that will make me reach out to God and my neighbor. May your mercy forgive the hard-heartedness which prevents me from loving freely.

SATURDAY OF THE THIRD WEEK OF LENT

Luke18:9-14

"O God, be merciful to me a sinner."

The times are hard and the scare from the CoViD-19 pandemic stares us in the face.

Many are the people who spend their days in fear, trepidation, and anxiety. Many more continue to dread the spread of the virus as they see infected cases grow exponentially each day. Many families around the world have been struck heavily and are mourning the loss of relatives and friends to this deadly virus. Today, we live in fear and panic, we live like strangers to one another. We are afraid to shake each other's hands, we dare not embrace one another, let alone give each other the kiss of peace. Like the proverbial biblical leper, one has to virtually ring a bell to announce one's presence and observe a decent social distance, so as to avoid possible infection. We have all been relegated to the confines of our small corners to quarantine in order not to infect or be infected. Our physical access to the sacraments has been diminished and our churches and streets have become ghost towns. This virus has brought the world to her knees as the world's economies keep tumbling and stocks continue to plummet. We are bruised like reeds. We are smoldered like wicks. The luster in our eyes is gone. We have been humbled and all our pride is gone.

In the face of all these, my question is, how did we come this far? How could the world with all its scientific strides be hit this hard without any immediate rapid antidote? Where did we go wrong? What sin did we commit? Did our fathers eat the sour grapes and set our teeth on edge?

As a matter of fact, this pandemic could be a cause for somber reflection. Today, Jesus tells the story of the Pharisee and the Publican who went up to pray. The former prayed as if everything depends on him and God is only his audience. The latter, keeping his distance, bowed, beat his breast and prayed as if everything including his very self depended on God. The former, in self-deception, prayed, numbering his achievements without regard to God's grace, whiles the latter, in self-awareness of his limitations, counted nothing of his achievements worth mentioning in the sight of God. The former prayed to spurn the latter, the latter prayed, beating himself for his sins and counting on God's mercy.

C. S. Lewis once said that humility is not thinking less of yourself, it's thinking of yourself less. The Pharisee thought more of himself and less of all others so he went home unjustified. The Publican thought of himself less and recognized his need for God's mercy, and Jesus said of him that his prayer was heard and he went away justified. His attitude to prayer smacks of the fact that sinners are not in the arms of an angry God but are in the warm embrace of a Father who is loving, merciful, kind and forgiving. His prayer is short but sincere. At prayer, he cleansed his mind and heart and opened up his being to receive God's Mercy.

Perhaps, for a long time, we have lived our lives as if the world spins around us. We have sold our consciences and have thought more of ourselves and less of God and others. Perhaps like the Pharisee we got the fundamentals wrong and made God a mere spectator in our endeavors. May these trying times send us all up to pray. The attitude of the Publican must be ours too. Let's keep a decent social distance from God, bow our heads in humble prayer and echo his words: O God, be merciful to me a sinner. This is the time to make a humble return to the Lord and ask him to bind our wounds and heal us. My belief is that if all of us would return to the Lord in humble prayer and repeat nothing but the prayer of the Publican, peace will reign in our hearts and the joy of the Lord shall be our strength.

My Jesus, my fear in the face of CoViD-19 is palpable. Feel my heartbeats and in your clemency enlighten our scientist to find an antidote to this global puzzle which has brought our world to its knees. Heal this world and make it a better place to live. Lord, be merciful to me a sinner.

MONDAY OF THE FOURTH WEEK OF LENT

John 4:43-54

"Sir, come down before my child dies."

Jesus heals, he heals from a distance.

Many of us have been saddened by the fact that the corona scare has kept us away from the Church and the sacraments. In our bid to nip the rapid spread of the virus in the bud and stem the mass extermination of humanity, a lockdown in many countries has affected the way we would all want to worship God. I have followed many arguments on social media ranging from the infringement on the individual's fundamental right to worship to the comparison of the bread we purchase from grocery stores to the bread of life in the Eucharist. The times are hard and the CoViD-19 emergency is real, so we all have good reasons to worry and to find solace in God's presence and his providence. Our need for Jesus in times as desperate as this has been heightened and it is understandable that people get frustrated who cannot access their orthodox means of reaching out to God. However, even when we cannot reach out to him the way we are used to, he can meet us wherever we are. He can throw his graces and mercies at us wherever we find ourselves. All we need is to pray.

Today we read the story of the royal official who accosted Jesus and begged him to come to heal his son. This official amazes me because of where he is coming from. In his capacity as a royal official, he most likely hails from the household of Herod Antipas, the tetrarch of Galilee and Perea, the same man who ordered John the Baptist executed. Despite his privileged position in society and although he could incur the displeasure of his boss or his boss' mistress, he comes anyway. Like any parent, he would risk anything to save his dying son. He comes to Jesus, not because he has faith in Jesus but because Jesus could work a miracle for him. In his mind, the only way his son could be healed was Jesus' physical presence in his house. Thus, when Jesus seemed to delay, he persists in asking Jesus to come quickly lest his son would die. Even when Jesus rebuked his lack of faith and suggested that like many others, he was only seeking signs and wonders, he makes no resistance. All he focuses on is to get Jesus home so his son would heal. His humility, his persistence, his courage to come to Jesus in a prayer of petition for his son is quite remarkable. What he didn't know was that Jesus could answer his prayer from a distance. He did not need Jesus' physical presence in his house for his son to be healed. Jesus, the Lord of life, is capable of throwing his love, his mercies, and his healing our way even from a distance and that is what he did. He said to the royal official, "You may go; your son will live." From Galilee, he reached out his healing power to the royal official's son in Capernaum. He did not need to make the journey there. God cannot be limited to specified locations. He is everywhere, his spirit and loving-kindness, his abiding presence is constantly with us and can be felt by all his children despite their location.

Like the royal official, let us come to him in humble prayer, let us persist in calling on him. Our encounters with him in the Eucharist could be truncated, yet our faith that he is everywhere, he knows everything, he sees all, and is even aware of our inmost thoughts should drive us to rely on him.

Even as he sends his healing from a distance, he also sets us an example, that our kindness to one another could also be activated from a distance. These are times when people staying at home and alone could easily get depressed and suicidal. They are times when people could lose their livelihoods and be despaired. May our own kind generosity reach out to all our friends, neighbors, and relatives wherever they are. Sometimes, it takes just a phone call, an email, a card, or a text message. A kind heart, they say, always makes a way. Just as Jesus made a way for his healing power to reach the royal official's son from a distance, may our own kindness cut across distances and bring solace and relief to someone who is in dire need of it. A friend in need is said to be a friend indeed.

Today, Jesus is reaching out to us in his love, mercy, and kindness. Let us also find out one another, be on the lookout for each other, and even from a distance give each other a hand so we can win this fight together. God be our help.

My Jesus, even when the royal official reached out to you with inadequate faith, you brought healing to his son from a distance. I come to you in all my limitations asking you to increase me in faith. Touch my life with your love and make me an instrument of your generosity, so that through me you can reach out to my needy brothers and sisters even from a distance.

TUESDAY OF THE FOURTH WEEK OF LENT

John 5:1-3, 5-16

"Do you want to be well?"

God made us for good. In the beginning, when God made everything he had made, he saw it all and it was good. Further on, he made man and saw that man is very good. Just as the crab never begets a bird, good should naturally beget good. As soon as man who has been made very good begins to deviate from the good and begins to give the wrong responses to the right questions of his existence, man extracts himself from God and avails himself for war with evil.

Take time to reflect on the human situation. All that the Lord God made was good. Man who was given the mandate to govern the earth and to till it was also given the privilege to use his ingenuity to employ something of what God had made to promote his wellbeing. Thus plants and animals were given us for victuals and for the promotion of the common good. Because the human condition poses many existential questions, the human person takes initiatives to use God's creation to respond to some of the decisive questions human nature poses. To travel long distances man's fitting response was the automobile, the ship, the airplane. To cure sicknesses and diseases, man's scientific findings manufacture medications by means of God's creation. Incidentally history teaches us that anytime we gave the wrong answers to the questions of the human situation, we gave ourselves away. Let us take time to do some reflection: How did we come by HIV and AIDS? How did we come by Ebola and SARS? And how have we come by CoViD-19? These are all results of the wrong responses we gave to the existential questions life poses. Life brings us many challenges and it is incumbent on us to join hands with God to find solutions to them. As soon as we lose sight of the fact that God made us for himself and that we must depend on him and allow him to let his goodness operate in us, something else takes the center stage which drives us to the wrong responses that land us in for disaster.

Today, we encounter the story of the cripple who for thirty-eight years had been struggling to get into the Bethesda to be healed. It beats my mind that he laid by the lake of mercy for 38 years and yet no one was merciful enough to help him into the pool for cleansing. Having suffered affliction for 38 years, he definitely wanted and needed to be cured. Yet when he encountered Jesus, he gave a deviated answer to the fitting question Jesus posed. Jesus' obvious question was: "Do you want to be well?" The paralytic's answer was: "Sir, I have no one to put me into the pool when the water is stirred up; while I am on my way, someone else gets down there before me." I believe the best answer he should have given was, "Yes, Sir. I want to be well." Yet, perhaps, out of frustration or because he had grown used to his predicament or because he was angry with all who had the speed to jump past him into the pool for a cure, he gave an answer to suggest that even in the sight of Jesus he still had hope in people who had failed him for 38 years. Jesus could have looked at his hope and his answer and left him to his fate. Yet God as he is and God, being good, Jesus took steps to restore him to good health. He did so without any critique and without any fanfare. He said to the paralytic, "Rise, take up your mat, and walk." Immediately the man became well, took up his mat, and walked." Our God is good. Even when we have wrong answers to the existential questions of life, he looks beyond our limitations and viciousness and makes all things new and beautiful in his time.

Friends, we may not know exactly if this pandemic is another wrong answer to some of the right questions life brings. Neither do we know if it is a result of some vitiation in the goodness of man. All the same, it has some lessons worth considering; life is full of choices. We are condemned to choose. Even if we fail to choose, our failure to do so is itself a choice we have made. We are responsible for our choices, yet our choices do not affect us alone. In this global village where we live, we all need to beware and realize that when we stretch our arms, they end where another person's nose begins. That if care is not taken we end up blowing off someone else's nose. Our freedom ends where another person's freedom begins. We should be careful what answers we give to the questions life brings. We should also mind the motivations behind our response to certain existential questions. If we allow ourselves to be driven by afflictions, frustrations, envy, jealousy, anger on account of others or the ego, we are likely to goof terribly and suffer the ill consequences of our actions and we will suffer with other innocent people. Any ball we throw against the wall bounces back at us.

The beauty in all this is that even when our unfitting answers have warranted our neglect form God, God always comes to our aid and works for our good. The paralytic's answer was a deviation but Jesus still asked him to rise, pick his pieces together and walk. CoVid could be another evil goofy response to one of the many questions of our existence. Yet God is still God. May He see beyond our depravity and ask us to rise up, take up our mats and walk. By his divine intervention, may we all be made well physically, emotionally, and psychologically. May all that the world goes through today unite our hearts to fear the name of him who alone has the power to save us.

My Jesus, as the world continues to fight this pandemic, I am consoled that your word keeps reminding me of your power to heal. Build my faith in you as the source of all health and enable me to take refuge in you who alone has the power and the goodwill to save me.

WEDNESDAY OF THE FOURTH WEEK OF LENT

John 5:17-30

"My Father is at work until now, so I am at work."

At the pool of Mercy, the crippled lay for 38 years with no one showing him mercy. Jesus came along and asked him to pick up his mat and walk. The man was immediately made well and as he walked around, the Jews said he was doing what was unlawful on the sabbath, carrying his mat around. The healed man declared his innocence and pointed to the one who healed him to have instructed him to pick up his mat and walk. The logic of events here is that it was the sabbath and the said healer had indirectly and directly broken the Law. Indirectly, he had commanded the crippled to do the unlawful on the Sabbath. It is a sin to command another to sin. So Jesus sinned by commanding the crippled to pick up his mat and walk. Directly, he himself had healed on the sabbath. To heal is to work. To work is to break the sabbath. Jesus had asked the crippled to work on the Sabbath. He had also healed to contravene God's law. As if that was not enough, when he was confronted with it, he said, "My Father is at work until now, so I am at work." Not only had he made himself equal to God the Father, but he was also citing God to be the breaker of his own law on the Sabbath. God is not a contradiction in himself. And he who shows himself as God only to contradict God is an imposter and a blasphemer. No wonder their desire to kill him grew more intense. He had doubly broken the law and was blaspheming God. He only deserved to die.

Yet in this episode, Jesus teaches an eternal truth. At the pool of mercy, the man in need may find no love and no mercy, yet God's love and mercy so abound and are so much at play that God doesn't mind breaking his own law to restore life and health to his own image and likeness. Even in his moment of rest, the maintenance and preservation of human life are so crucial to God that God will let loose his love and mercy, where they are lacking, to embrace us and make us whole. The healing of the cripple at the pool of Siloam thus teaches us that God's grace and mercy operate as graciously as would defy God's law when life is at stake. It does not matter the day of the week, God's gracious love and abounding mercy will meet us at our point of need when we turn to him. Human life is more important to God than the letter of the law and God will overrule his law and save us if we turn to him at our point of need.

My God, in the time of trouble, when I turn to you, may your abounding love and mercy bring me comfort.

Thursday Of The Fourth Week Of Lent

John 5:31-47

"But I have testimony greater than John's. The works that the Father gave me to accomplish, these works that I perform testify on my behalf that the Father has sent me."

Perhaps we have heard this question before: What are your credentials? Or where are your credentials?

A credential is ordinarily a testimony given by another.

According to the dictionary, it is a qualification, an achievement, a personal quality, or an aspect of a person's background, typically when used to indicate that they are suitable for something. Sometimes it is a document or certificate proving a person's identity or qualifications. Politically speaking, a credential is a letter of introduction given by a government to an ambassador before a new posting.

However, etymologically, the word credential originates from the Latin credo, credere, meaning I believe, or to believe. It implies something I have which makes people believe that I am what I say I am. It is not necessarily something coming from another but something originating from me. That which is so intrinsically part of me that all who encounter me can not help but testify that I am true to what I claim I am. That issuing forth from within me which testifies to my credibility- that is my credential. When

Jesus died on the Cross the centurion standing in front of him saw how he gave his last breath and said: "Truly this man is the son of God!" The centurion needed no testimony other than what he saw to testify that Jesus is the son of God. If a credential is a testimony, it is one which issues forth from what I am and what I portray by my way of life. My credentials are the history I write with my life which comes to judge me accordingly.

Today, Jesus contends with the Jews about his credentials. In his life, there were three authentic testimonies to his identity. John the Baptist testified to the truth. He was loud and clear, This is the Lamb of God. I am not fit to unstrap his sandals. He must increase and I must decrease. The Father also testified to him, "This is my beloved son in whom I am well pleased." The scriptures also testified to him. Yet they wouldn't believe. Jesus argues that even though John was light and they contented in his light, they failed to believe John's testimony. They believed in the Father. All the same, the Father's testimony didn't ring a bell. They searched through scripture which they believed would save them. Yet they did not subscribe to Moses' testimony on him. But he has his own credentials: "The works that the Father gave me to accomplish, these works that I perform testify on my behalf that the Father has sent me." Jesus seems to be saying that the best of humans could testify on your behalf, even God and his word could do so, yet, if people make their minds not to believe in you they will not believe. The best credential, therefore, is the one we write as we do the will of God. How we attend to the works, the professions and vocations we have been called to, the accomplishments we make, the way we order ourselves in those accomplishments determine what we have for which others must believe in us.

As a priest, my credentials must not be in the ordination certificate or a letter of suitability. As a doctor or a nurse, my credentials must not be in the board certification. As an attorney, my credentials must not be the certificate that called me to the bar. As a journalist, my credentials lie not in sensationalism but the truth I churn out to the world even as I disseminate information. As a teacher, my credentials are more in the love and the passion I bring to my duties than the teacher's certificate. As a husband or a wife, my credentials must not be in the marriage certificate.

In this life, we are all writing our histories. The history we write testifies on our behalf. If we write a good history it will come to judge us accordingly. If we write a bad one it will equally judge us. What do I have which will make others believe in what I claim to be? What history am I writing for myself even as I go about my Master's business daily?

My Jesus, you came into the world not to count on human testimony. Through the accomplishment of your Father's will, you showed yourself His son. May I follow in your footsteps and faithfully do the will of God so as to write a history that will judge me aright at the end of time.

Friday Of The Fourth Week Of Lent

John 7: 1-2, 10, 25-30

"You know me and also know where I am from."

The problem of knowledge has been a battle that philosophers have fought since the beginnings of time. Many a time, people mistake opinion for knowledge. Other times mere beliefs, prejudices, misconceptions and perceptions are misconstrued as knowledge. In the history of civilization, people are known to have dwelt on their belief-less and untrue stereotyping perceptions to end the lives and carriers of others. I have come across intelligent elites who have tenaciously entertained falsehoods as knowledge and have defended them publicly to the detriment of others and their livelihoods. Listen to many a political discourse today and it will take you no time to realize how much we stand up for things we think we know but do not in reality know. How many of our political leaders have we not been maligned and booted out of office all because of the falsehood their opponents fabricated around them? Many innocent lives have been destroyed because of falsehood and many a talent has been killed out of ignorance.

It was thus not out of place that at his time, Plato sought to define knowledge as justified true belief. According to him, if I should say that I know that something is the case, I must first have a belief, my belief must be founded and true, and I should have a good reason for holding that belief. For Plato, belief, truth, and justification must necessarily be present for one to claim knowledge and if these three ingredients are available, then one indeed has knowledge.

Today we are told that Jesus moved about within Galilee; he did not wish to travel in Judea, because the Jews were trying to kill him. The question is, Why were the Jews trying to kill Jesus? They were trying to kill him because they thought they knew who he was. He was a mere carpenter's son posing as the Christ. He was a mere man equating himself to God. They thought they knew him but they did not. Actually, the Jews entertained a mere false belief about Jesus and they mistook their unfounded belief for knowledge. Therefore, when they thought they had knowledge of Jesus and where he came from, they were only living in ignorance.

Not only were the Jewish leaders ignorant, but the people also proved themselves so. Some of the inhabitants of Jerusalem said, "Is he not the one they are trying to kill? And look, he is speaking openly and they say nothing to him. Could the authorities have realized that he is the Christ? But we know where he is from. When the Christ comes, no one will know where he is from." Here, the inhabitants also thought they knew Jesus, they thought they knew where Jesus is from but in actual fact they didn't and Jesus knew that they were also ignorant.

They may, out of ignorance want to kill Jesus but the truth must stand. So, much as he didn't wish to go to Judah, he seized the opportunity of the Feast of the Tabernacles to go and set the records straight. He cried out in the temple area and said, "You know me and also know where I am from. Yet I did not come on my own, but the one who sent me, whom you do not know, is true. I know him because I am from him, and he sent me."

Here Jesus lays down his true identity. He is the One whom the Father sent. If the Father loved the world so much that he gave his only begotten son, then Jesus is the Son of God, Jesus is the Messiah. The more he made this truth clear to the Jews, the more they wanted him dead, because in their ignorance they took him for an imposter. In all this, Jesus was never bitter, neither was he mad at them. If he had anything in his heart for them, it was love and forgiveness. It is therefore understandable that from the cross Jesus would pray, saying, "Father, forgive them for they do not know what they are doing."

How often have I acted on mere belief without taking time to examine it for truth and justification? How many toes have I stepped on because I was so set in my false beliefs that I failed to give the truth a fighting chance to operate? Out of ignorance, we can destroy. Out of ignorance, we can kill. Out of ignorance, we can discriminate against others. Out of ignorance, we can deny others their rights and relegate others to the dungeons. Out of ignorance, our world has brought innocent people to the gallows and many have been made to suffer the bad consequences of our prejudices. However, it takes the patience and confidence of Jesus (devoid of anger and bitterness) to lead people out of ignorance into the wonderful light of true belief which is duly justified.

My Jesus, today, may it never happen that someone will suffer because of my ignorance and if I should suffer on account of someone else's ignorance, may I be granted the serenity to know the difference and never grow bitter.

SATURDAY OF THE FOURTH WEEK OF LENT

John 7: 40-53

"Does our law condemn a man before it first
hears him and finds out what he is doing?"

My favorite definition of law I got from St. Thomas Aquinas. In his Treatise on Law, he defines law as an ordinance of reason for the common good, promulgated by him who has care of the community. This definition of law suggests a number of things: viz., that law is a command and not a mere counsel. It is obligatory and binding. It flows not from the will of a leader but is a product of reason, a well thought out instrument which does not originate from the whims and caprices of the leader. It is for the good of all. If it benefits an individual, it is because the individual interest is also the interest of the community. Law, therefore, must be binding, it ought to be reasonable, it must be community serving, must come from a competent authority and must be made manifest to all. One thing about the law is that it does not bind only the ruled it also binds the ruler. Therefore no one is above the law.

Today, we encounter diverse reactions to Jesus. The crowd heard him and concluded that he was indeed a prophet. Others said he was the Christ. The guards who were sent to arrest him were fascinated by his teaching. They felt no one spoke as convincingly as Jesus did and so didn't have the courage to arrest him. The Jewish leaders were contemptuous. Without hearing Jesus, they concluded he was guilty and ought to die.

They rubbished the testimony of the crowd as coming from some accursed bunch of people, who were so good for nothing that no one needed to pay them any attention, let alone count on their testimony to make a decision on Jesus. They continued to argue to the effect that Jesus was not qualified to be the Christ as the Christ should hail from Bethlehem and not Galilee. If Jesus was Jesus of Nazareth, then any claim that he was the Christ is blasphemous and per the law, blasphemy attracts nothing but condemnation. Nicodemus followed the trend of events and realizing that they were operating outside the confines of the law, reminded them that their law does not condemn a man unless it first hears his case and has first-hand information of what he is doing. In other words, the law calls for justice and justice demands that no one is deemed guilty until he is proven so. Thus Nicodemus reminded the house that until they took steps to prove Jesus guilty, Jesus was innocent. What is happening here is that the leaders of the community were taking the law into their own hands. They were acting as if they were above the law and they could shelve all due processes in regard to the law and deal with Jesus. They wouldn't buy the witness coming from the crowd, they wouldn't also accept the testimony of the guards, neither would they set the stage for Jesus to defend his claim. They willed power, they interpreted the law, they knew it all, the Messiah must come from Bethlehem. Jesus hails from Galilee. A Galilean claiming to be the Christ is a usurper and anyone who claims and grasps equality with God must be condemned. Jesus must thus be condemned. They took the law into their own hands. They cared only about themselves. They were myopic in their judgment of Christ. The common interest, the benefits Jesus brought to the crowds, the impact he made on the guards were all not worth considering. They operated from their wills without giving reason a chance. Because they had made their minds up to condemn Jesus without examining the facts, they ridiculed their colleague and without wanting to face the truth which came from Nicodemus, they dispersed. They dispersed only to abort justice and to put Jesus to death on the cross. Well, theirs was the loss for aborting justice but ours was the gain because it is in his death that we have our salvation. If they meant it for evil, God meant it for God.

Today, my heart goes out to the many around the world who have been unjustly condemned and those convicted without any fair trial. People society deemed guilty when they had not been proven so. People to whom instant justice was meted out and lynched for things they never did. Those who were falsely accused and condemned without any Nicodemus to prick the conscience of the powers that be. I also pray for people who will power and authority in society, our legislators and law enforcement agents, those who interpret the law and those who execute it, that far from operating by the dictates of their whims and caprices, they would be driven by right reason and the common good so that justice will be promoted and peace will reign in our world and in our hearts.

My Jesus, grant me the grace to be circumspect in my judgement of others. May I never either bear any false witness against my neighbor or rashly condemn anyone especially when I am not privy to the whole truth.

MONDAY OF THE FIFTH WEEK OF LENT

John 8:1-11

"Then the scribes and the Pharisees brought a woman who
had been caught in adultery and made her stand in the middle.
They said to him, "Teacher, this woman was caught in the
very act of committing adultery. Now in the law, Moses
commanded us to stone such women. So what do you say?"

If one commits adultery, then the one must die. This woman was caught
in the very act of committing adultery, therefore she must die. This biblical
passage proposes a logical argument form known as the Modus Ponens.
What is left unsaid would constitute another form of a logical argument
which will land Jesus in a dilemma. Anyone confronted with such an
argument form faces a dilemma. In the case of Jesus, the dilemma was
whether to condemn the woman to be stoned or to vindicate and exonerate
her from the death penalty. If Jesus is the face of the Father's mercy, then
condemning the woman would undermine his claim for compassion. If
he exonerates her, he stands to break the law of Moses and encourages
adultery. Either he undermines his claim for mercy and compassion or he
presents himself as a breaker of the law. If he encourages adultery, he would
contradict himself. For he had said before, that whoever breaks the law
and teaches others to do the same would be called least in the kingdom of
God and the Son of God cannot be least in his Father's Kingdom. Imagine
a compassionate Savior condemning a daughter of Abraham to death, or
the Messiah breaking the Law of Moses. Either way, Jesus would lose.
Therefore, what seemed a promotion of the Law of God, was rather a trap

for Jesus. The Jewish leaders are out to get at him and they didn't care about using a fellow human being as bait.

In the face of the dilemma, what were Jesus' options? He could do 3 things: 1. to tackle the dilemma by the horns. 2. To escape through the horns and 3. To put up a new argument. What did Jesus do? We are told he stooped to write in the sand and as the people pressed on, he rose and said: "Let the one among you who is without sin be the first to throw a stone at her." Jesus could have tacked the dilemma by the horns by inquiring about the details of the adulterous act. I am imagining how a woman who was caught in an adulterous act, could act alone. Yet Jesus did not. Perhaps doing so would have put the man also en route for death, but he had come to give life and give it to the full. What Jesus did was to escape through the horns. His argument with the people was that the woman had sinned indeed but since there were some, if not all, in the crowd who had themselves sinned and were still alive, that same mercy which was keeping them alive must keep the poor woman alive too. Jesus did not condone the sin of the woman, he only used the eye of an elder to look into the darkness of the woman's life and gave her a chance to live and a chance for change, just as God had given all those stone-wielding men a chance to live despite their many sins.

Friends, this story gingers many questions. Why did Jesus stoop to write in the sand? Was the woman alone when she was caught in the very act of adultery? Should a fellow human being be used as a means to an end?

Scott Hurd opines that Jesus stooped to write in the sand to give the people the time to think through what they were about to do to the woman. As Jesus traced his fingers in the sand, he was teaching the crowd the need to take time to think before they impulsively cast a stone at another. How often have I not rashly allowed my anger, my emotions, and my prejudices to lead the way in my assessment of others in given situations! Today Jesus writes in the sand too and he intends to ask you and me to take some time to examine people's situations and circumstances before we judge and condemn them. Sometimes it is necessary to allow time to number our own mercies received in the face of our sins and excesses and show equal mercy to others. This woman had sinned, yes! But would putting her to death have been the only and best solution at the time? I don't think so.

The woman was caught in the very act of adultery. One may ask, where was the man? Perhaps he was too strong for them to arrest so they arrested the weaker of the two and presented her for execution. See how often society favors the strong and condemns the weak. See how often certain figures in society are given preferential treatment over others because they are rather well off than others. Whenever we failed to protect the interest of the poor, the needy, and the weak in society, we are like the crowd who brought only this woman up to be stoned.

Why did they want to use a fellow human being to trap Jesus and condemn him? Does it strike you that we often do the same? It is easy to use another person or their situation just to get a favor or something we want. Friends have betrayed friends just to achieve their ambitions. Trusts have been betrayed simply because someone in the contract had something to gain and didn't care if the other had everything to lose. We turn to use other people as objects to get to our selfish ends and whenever we did we were not better than the folks who tried to use this woman to trap Jesus.

Today, we are invited to allow ourselves some time to think through our actions before we take them.

If society is unfair to the weak, let's not join the crowd.

Let's treat other people as subjects and not as objects.

Jesus came that we may have life to the full. He will never take any action that would truncate life. Let us all promote life and encourage others to do the same.

My Jesus, you did not condemn the sinful woman to die but rather gave her another chance to live and to sin no more. When my own sins are many and overwhelming, may your mercy grant me another chance to live as your grace affords me the courage to eschew sin.

TUESDAY OF THE FIFTH WEEK OF LENT

John 8:21-30

"When you lift up the Son of Man, then you will realize that I AM"

Semiology is the philosophy of signs. It is that branch of philosophy that studies signs, symbols, and meaning. According to this philosophy, every sign or symbol has a double meaning- a denotation and a connotation. A sign's denotation is simply what the sign is. For instance, a stop sign is what it is, it is a road sign. That is what it denotes. A sign's connotation refers to the meaning associated with it. So the stop sign would mean something more than a mere road sign, something more than meets the eye. For these philosophers, a sign is polysemic, that is to say, a sign could connote diverse meanings, depending on a person's worldview, background and culture. The denotative and connotative concepts of signs thus suggest that signs and symbols point to a certain reality that might not be immediately realized and the reality they point to could be diverse. Signs are also pointers to reality and not imagination. If something is a sign or a symbol then it is not empty, it is replete with meaning, it directs to reality out there. A symbol has a meaning. It is a reminder of a fact and reality.

Like all signs and symbols, the Cross is a sign. When Emperor Constantine sought a sign for victory from God, he was shown the Cross in his vision and was told, " In this sign, you will conquer." The Cross of Jesus is, therefore, a sign, it is a symbol and like all symbols, it is replete with meaning and is a pointer to Reality. Generally speaking, the Cross is known as a symbol of our salvation, a symbol of self-sacrifice, humility, love, forgiveness, and hard work.

Today, Jesus underscores the polysemic effect of the Cross and gives us another meaning to the Cross. But before we examine Jesus' teaching here, permit me to bring you a little back to the episode of the burning bush. Moses makes an encounter with God by the burning bush in the desert and God sends him to Egypt to liberate his people. He demands to know God's name and God tells him, " When you go, tell the people that I AM sent you." God's name, therefore, is I AM.

In today's gospel, Jesus tells the Jews, "...if you do not believe that I AM, you will die in your sins." So they said to him, "Who are you?" His answer among others is, "When you lift up the Son of Man, then you will realize that I AM." How was Jesus lifted up? He was lifted up on the cross. His answer could consequently be re-stated as: When you lift up the Son of Man on the Cross, then you will realize that I AM. Jesus is here saying that in the Cross is the manifestation and the realization of his divinity. The Cross symbolizes that Jesus is God. If God's name is I AM and Jesus' mounting the Cross will let the world know that I AM, then what God is, Jesus also is. Jesus is God and the Cross is a pointer to that reality. We know our God by the mystery of the Cross. We realize he is God because Jesus died on the cross.

Friends, at our baptism we were marked with the sign of the Cross. This indicates our acceptance of this symbol and what it stands for. It also indicates our share in it. By the Cross, we accept Jesus as our Lord and God. By the Cross, we acknowledge our dependence on God in this life's journey. Whenever I carry my own individual cross, I should carry it in the light of Jesus' Cross and come to make an encounter with God. The Cross of CoViD-19 which we bear today should enable us to realize our God, make a return to him and see His hand at work in the twists and turns of life's events. Every Cross I encounter in life should ultimately lead me to encounter God and know him more deeply and love him more dearly.

In the shadows of the Cross, we are saved. In the shadows of the Cross, we conquer, in the shadows of the Cross we learn the humility and obedience of Christ. Beneath the wings of the Cross, God's love binds us all in his warm embrace. Above all at the foot of the Cross, we come to the knowledge that Jesus Christ is God indeed.

My Jesus, in the mystery of the Cross, you manifest your greatness, you unveil your divinity. When our toil with the burden of CoViD-19 is done may we all grow to acknowledge you as our Lord and Saviour, the Alpha and Omega. May we give you the glory which is due to your name.

WEDNESDAY OF THE FIFTH WEEK OF LENT

John 8:31-42

"So if the Son frees you, then you will truly be free."

Freedom has been variously defined. For Pythagoras, to be free is to be the master of the self. For Socrates, free is the one who has rule over his pleasures. Plato saw freedom in the opportunity to be raised in the ideal State and have the values of the polity inculcated in you. For Aristotle, the free person is one who has the right use of reason, the ability to direct himself, and the capacity to participate in the governance of the polity. For the Greeks generally, freedom was Responsibility, responsibility towards others and oneself. Inherent in their concept of freedom was the principle of autonomy, the ability to self-rule. When the ingredient of autonomy was overly stretched, freedom degenerated in certain quarters and was taken to mean the capacity to live outrageously without any regard for the other. Freedom thus became a freely contested term.

The Jews also had a view of freedom. They defined freedom per their relationship with Abraham. Thus, to be a descendant, a son or a daughter of Abraham is to be free. It is for this reason that they would say to Jesus, "We are descendants of Abraham and have never been enslaved to anyone. How can you say, 'You will become free'?" What they failed to realize was that Abraham was free because his faith was credited to him as righteousness. Jesus reminded them that though they claimed to be slaves to no one, they were slaves to sin. In his words, "Amen, amen, I say to you, everyone who commits sin is a slave of sin." Being slaves to sin, they had no place in the Father's house and so the only one who can grant them entry is the Son who alone has the right of inheritance in the Father's house. For Jesus then, the free person is not a son or a daughter of Abraham but a son or daughter of God. Freedom is not in Abraham, freedom is rather in God. However because the sons and daughters of God have abused their freedom and have enslaved themselves to sin, the one who can really set them free is the Son.

With this, Jesus throws light on his original statement that if they remained in his word, they would be his disciples, they would know the truth and the truth will set them free.

St. John tells us at the beginning of his gospel that, in the beginning, was the Word, the Word was with God, the Word was God and the Word became flesh and dwelt among us. Jesus is the Word made flesh. To dwell in his word is to dwell in him. Therefore, whoever dwells in the word of Jesus dwells in Jesus himself. Jesus is the Son of God's household who can truly set the slave of sin free. He is the way and the truth. To dwell in Jesus and be his disciple is to imbibe the truth which Jesus is and it is this truth that sets the sinner free and returns him to God's household, where he truly belongs and has true freedom. For Jesus therefore, to be free is to dwell in him.

Today, many people see freedom as a license to do what they want. Quite often, we even hear people quote the scriptures and say, "Don't I have the right to do what I want with my own money?" Freedom has thus become to many the right to do what one wants and often it is so considered without regard to infringing on other people's freedom. Freedom so considered is no respecter of truth, it considers only the self and the will. It closes its eye to right reason. It embraces desired pleasure and makes its attainment a right. It assumes autonomy, the kind that can willfully infringe on other people's rights without qualms. It is devoid of discipline and tends to eventual self-incapacitation. In the end, when we think we are free, we realize we never really are. We are rather slaves to selfishness and sin. And as slaves to selfishness and sin, we lose our inheritance in the Father's house. Jesus alone is our refuge, he alone is our salvation, he alone can set us free from the fetters that bog us down. He is the Son who can liberate us all. All we need is to abide in him and his word and allow him to school us in his truth and let his truth break the chains of our imprisonment.

My Jesus, when my erroneous sense of freedom rather places me in the fetters of sin, may you let me evermore abide in your Word and your truth which alone can enlighten my path and lead me home to your Father's house where true freedom abounds.

THURSDAY OF THE FIFTH WEEK OF LENT

John 8:51-59

Amen, amen, I say to you, whoever keeps
my word will never see death."

Theologians identify three forms of life and death. According to them, there is Physical life and physical death. Physical life is the life we acquire from birth. It is the life we have when we can breathe, and move and have our being. Physical death is the termination of physical life. It is the separation of soul and body. All the lockdown, social distancing, and face masking we are experiencing in the face of CoViD-19 are aimed at maintaining physical life and averting physical death. Yet when the day of toil is done and the race of life is run, dust will surely return to dust and ashes to ashes and mortal man will cease to exist in his physical self.

There is also Spiritual life and Spiritual death. Spiritual life, according to theologians is the life of the soul that is open to and united with sanctifying grace. A life that is open to God and has the promise of eternal life. It is a life that is blessed because it lives the beatitudes and is lived in constant union with God and his word. Spiritual death, on the other hand, occurs when the soul is separated from God and his infused grace. This separation comes not from God but the devil. In the Garden of Eden, Adam and Eve hid from God because the serpent tricked them into disobedience. There is also Eternal life and eternal death. Eternal life is the fruition of spiritual life. When my life of sanctity germinates and matures when my soul opens up to sanctifying grace and lives in perpetual union with God and his word

Jesus grants me an abode in his father's house. St Paul puts it beautifully when he says that we know that when our earthly dwelling is razed to the ground we have an abode in heaven that no human hands have made. The fruition of spiritual death is eternal death. To die eternally is to die in a state of Mortal sin. It is eternal separation from God. We believe that God did not create death and the destruction of human life. He formed man to be imperishable. However, the book of Wisdom tells us that it is by the envy of the devil that death came into the world, and those who are on his side suffer it. Eternal death is thus the death of those who align themselves with the devil and thereby separate themselves eternally from God.

Today, Jesus makes an emphatic statement: whoever keeps my word will never see death. The Jews contend with him. Even Abraham died, so what on earth is he saying? As if that was not enough, he tells them that Abraham longed to see his days, but he is not yet fifty years of age. How could he have lived before Abraham? Then he makes the matter worse by saying that before Abraham was, I AM. His words are difficult to keep. He is not only placing himself above Abraham, he is equating himself to God. Who will keep his word? And since his word even seems blasphemous, they pick up stones to pelt at him. St. John tells us Jesus hid and went out of the temple area.

Friends, I think this was a very dark day in the lives of the Jews. They couldn't keep Jesus' word, they attempted to pelt him and Jesus hid and left the temple area. If Jesus is God, then because they failed to keep his word and wielded stones to pelt at him, God separated himself from them. God hid from them. That they failed to keep Jesus' word and made Jesus hide and leave the temple area is tantamount to saying that they died a spiritual death which culminated in eternal death. They failed to be imbued by the word of God, they failed to take grace which Jesus infused so they tasted death, perhaps they died eternally. As one theologian once said, the horror of hell is indeed not fire but the eternal absence of God. With Jesus leaving the temple area, God hid from them and distanced himself from their lives.

St. Augustine brilliantly comments on this passage and says that as a man Jesus fled from the stones, but woe to them from whose stony hearts God flies away. Today, when Jesus' words are hard to keep, we harden our hearts and deaden our consciences. We pelt him with our hard-heartedness and warped consciences. Some place God on the index of their life, treating him like a giant clockmaker who has set the clock of life into motion and has nothing more to do with it. Many more even kill God in their lives and turn his values upside down. They have deified themselves and claim to be a law unto themselves.

Today, we are reminded, there is life and there is death. The life which comes from dust should return to dust. But this life must be lived in keeping with God's Word. If we open up to God's Word, our souls are infused with graces from above which enable us to grow in union with God forever. On the contrary, if we harden our hearts and wield our hearts of stone in readiness to pelt at Jesus, he will hide and flee from the temple which we all are. May it never happen that our hardheartedness would separate us eternally from God. If today you hear his voice, harden not your heart.

My Jesus, incline my heart to be docile to your word. By the light and the promptings of this word may I be constantly united with you here on earth and so be eternally united with you in your father's house.

FRIDAY OF THE FIFTH WEEK OF LENT

John 10:31-42

"You, a man, are making yourself God"

Perhaps we all know quite well this story of King David and the Prophet Nathan. After David had sinned and covered up, Nathan proposed a riddle and asked David what he would do. The riddle suggested a rich man who upon all the many sheep he had, slaughtered a poor man's only lamb to entertain his guest. David was enraged by the riddle and outrightly concluded that that man must surely die. To his dismay, the prophet said to him, "That man is you."

Has it ever happened to you that you cited a fault in a friend and realized too late that what you accused in them featured rather prominently in you? When people's private sins become public, if we should mind the people who are loud and loquacious in condemnation, we would realize that they are rather the worse offenders, or perhaps they have more terrible weaknesses in their own closets. The African proverb is, therefore, true which says that when you point an accusing finger at another person, be wary, because there will always be three other fingers pointing back at you. In our own lives, it does not take us time to see how often we accused a sin in another which was also in us in full measure. It is therefore important that we took time to see, time to judge, time to reflect, before we acted on our judgments.

Today, the Jews are up in arms against Jesus. They are angrily wielding stones to mete out capital punishment to him. This is not the first time they are trying this. They tried this in John 8. They are trying it again in John 10. This time around, Jesus demands, "I have shown you many good works from my Father. For which of these are you trying to stone me?" Their answer is quite intriguing, "We are not stoning you for a good work but for blasphemy. You, a man, are making yourself God."

Jesus is the Son of God. He is the one the Father has consecrated and sent. At his baptism, the Spirit descended like a dove and the voice declared him as the beloved son in whom the Father is well-pleased. All his works: raising the dead, healing the sick, walking upon the sea, and calming the storms, point to the power of God in him. Yet when he alluded to what he truly is, the Jews take issue with him, accusing him of blasphemy, and are ready to execute him. Jesus reminds them that even though they were made little less than God, scripture permits them to be referred to as gods. As a matter of fact, their very conduct, the way they carried themselves about, all smacked of attempts at dethroning God. They were all-knowing, they were the epitome of the law, they judged and condemned, they secured places of honor in the synagogues, they considered others to be good only to be used as fuel for the fires of hell and wouldn't associate with people they considered sinners. Thus, they were blaming in Jesus what featured conspicuously in themselves: men, acting as and claiming to be what they are not, men claiming to be God. If anyone should be stoned to death, it should not be Jesus, because Jesus is God. If any should be arrested, they should be the culprits. They had acted like God when they actually are not.

Friends, sometimes we find ourselves in the shoes of the Jews. We are too quick to throw stones at others for what we perceive in them as their weaknesses. Yet we are the ones. We are too busy to think about our sins. We are so nervously busy that we do not remember our sins. I love myself, my own self. I am my own law. I determine what is right and what is wrong. I treat my neighbor as an inferior, as a means to my profit, a patent to my pleasure. I'm the end of my existence. And there is nothing more blasphemous than acting as God in my capacity. Remember, they wanted to stone Jesus because they thought he was a man claiming to be God. What they forgot was that they were themselves truly men made in the likeness of God who acted as if they were gods. What we accuse in others, we are most likely going to find in ourselves in bold relief. We do not see others as they are. We see them as we are.

Today, let's all be slow to judge but rich in compassion, for that man we judge and condemn could be us.

My Jesus, it is very easy for me to be uncharitable to others for their weaknesses. Open my eyes to my limitations and as you dispose me to be sorry for them, soften my heart that I may have empathy for them who are as weak as I am.

SATURDAY OF THE FIFTH WEEK OF LENT

John 11:45-57

"This man is performing many signs. If we leave him alone, all will believe in him, and the Romans will come and take away both our land and our nation."

Metaphysicians say that Good is appetizable. In other words, Good is desirable, Good attracts. Good never repels. If anything is unappetizable, it is evil, for evil is the privation of the good. This implies that every good thing, every good act naturally tends to draw people either to itself or to its source. If a good done or achieved fails to attract, then the said good most likely undermines a selfish interest or shoots people out of their comfort zone. When people do the best within their means to bring about the good and all they receive in return is criticism and hostilities it doesn't take time to realize that if indeed their acts are good, the hostilities issue from some bitterness that blinds thinking-men and women to the appetizability of the good. We hardly want to see our enemies or opponents chalk up feats. It is even more so when their feats and progress seem to undermine our selfish ambitions. For this reason, our world is filled with rancorous divisions. The matter gets even worse when it enters the political discourse. We taint the truth, we shade the good, we twist the facts, and all pretentiously in the name and the interest of the nation and for the common good.

Jesus raised Lazarus from death. Lazarus had been dead for four days. Jesus after praying to his Father shouts him out of the grave. Death could be cruel. When death lays its icy hands on a person, no human being can restore them to life. Thus to restore a man from the cruel grips of death at a time when his family was broken and shattered was indeed a good act. Good naturally attracts. Therefore, this act of Jesus should have attracted and gingered a movement in those who had come to mourn with Martha and Mary. We are told, as it should be expected, that many of the Jews who had seen what Jesus had done began to believe in him. These were attracted by the good to the Good. However, some of them went to the Pharisees and told them what Jesus had done. It is not clear what their motive was when they reported what Jesus had done to the Pharisees. Whatever their motive might have been, they welled up fear and insecurity in the Sanhedrin. Their power and honor were on the line. Jesus had to be stopped else all the people would believe in him, the Romans would smell insurrection and come to conquer their land and nation. One would expect that they would be carried over by the many good signs Jesus was working. So why are they rather concerned? What indeed was at stake was their places of honor, their threatened authority, their prestige, their comfort zone. Their fear of losing things they cherished, closed their eyes to the good Jesus was doing. They hid behind the common good, the common interest, and concluded that Jesus ought to die. To buttress their stand, they had a High priest prophesy that it was better for one man to die than for the whole nation to perish. Better to eliminate the source of good than to sit idly by to be kicked out of your comfort zone. Incidentally, when they thought they were protecting their bread, God was rolling out his master plan. Their evil machinations and designs prepared the grounds for our salvation. Good will always yield the good even if it is vilified in the process. Light will always overcome darkness even if darkness makes a momentary survival. Our God can bring good out of evil. These would hatch a plot to execute Jesus but by his wounds, we are healed; by his stripes, we are saved. Ours were the sufferings he bore. If the plot was to cover up the good he did, it rather paved the way for a higher good- the salvation of humanity, a thing of beauty, which has been the joy of humankind forever.

Friends, today we are invited to take time to delve into our prejudices, our bitterness against others, and the tendency to see evil even when good abounds.

We are again encouraged not to depart from doing what is right even if the good in us fails to attract anyone. Good will always be good and the truth will always stand.

We are also called to be authentic in our dealings with others. If we claim to have their interests at heart may it not be our hidden interests that we peruse.

May I not be seen to do good for me.

Let's appreciate the good in others even if we dislike them.

Our faith in God should grow, especially in hard times, because he can bring good out of bad situations.

My Jesus, when my self-centeredness blinds me to the good in others, may your kindness remove the scales from my eyes so I can appreciate the power of your hand at work in the people I encounter in life.

PALM SUNDAY

"The crowds preceding him and those following kept crying out and saying: "Hosanna to the Son of David; blessed is he who comes in the name of the Lord; hosanna in the highest.""

Today is Palm Sunday. It is also known as Passion Sunday. It marks the beginning of Holy Week. On this day, Christians over the world join in the procession, carrying branches to commemorate Jesus' regal entry into Jerusalem. Like the people of old, we sing Hosanna to the Son of David. The word hosanna is very relevant to the times we live in. For once in the history of the Church, the world is celebrating Palm Sunday while quarantined. The age-old traditions of Palm Sunday are only being marked on the screens. Our hearts break to think of celebrating the peaks of our faith in private and in silence. Yet, one cannot underestimate the reality of CoViD-19. It has launched such a vicious attack on humanity that countless host of people have lost their lives and its threats continue to loom. It is in the wake of this scare that I find Jesus' triumphal entry and passion relevant.

Hosanna was the song of the crowd. What does the word "Hosanna" mean?

According to Pope emeritus Benedict XVI, hosanna was originally a word of urgent supplication. It meant something like: Come to our aid! The priests would repeat it in a monotone on the seventh day of the Feast of Tabernacles, while processing seven times around the altar of sacrifice, as an urgent prayer for rain. Today, in the privacy of our hearts, we sing hosanna. We do so in supplication to the Lord. In our distress we call upon the Lord, we cry unto him hosanna, not in supplication for rains but in supplication for a cure and a restoration of peace and goodwill in our ranks and files. We sing hosanna in urgent supplication to our God who alone can heal the world and bring our lives back to normalcy. We sing hosanna in supplication to God to forgive our excesses, to pardon our weaknesses, and restore the peace we have forfeited.

Pope Benedict, further opines that as the Feast of Tabernacles gradually changed from a feast of petition into one of praise, the cry for help also turned more and more into a shout of jubilation. My belief is that our sorrows today would be turned into joys because the Lord in his mercy will hear our cry of supplication and take steps to take away this virus and its adverse effects. He makes all things beautiful in his time. So, very soon he shall act decisively and we shall smile at the storm and sing hosanna in praise and thanksgiving to God for the great things he has done and continues to do. Our hosanna today is, therefore, a cry of hope. We sing hosanna in the hope and faith that God will turn our mourning into dancing.

By the time of Jesus, the Pope continues, the word had acquired Messianic overtones. Singing hosanna to the son of David was an acknowledgment of him as the Messiah, the Christ who is to come. Hosanna to Jesus was to underline his Kingship. Jesus Christ is King, the universal King, the King who rides not a horse but a donkey. That the people picked up palm branches, spread their garments, and hailed him loud hosanna was a brilliant expression of their faith in him as their Prince of Peace.

Today we also sing hosanna and we do so praising God in faith that even in these trying times the hour of the Messiah has arrived. We sing hosanna also as a prayer that God's kingship over Our world should be reestablished. For some time now, our world has turned the tables upside down. We have dethroned God and have lawlessly departed from him. We have multiplied our sins and have rationalized our weaknesses. We have chosen to run our lives without any regard to his law. In our scientific exploits, God did not matter anymore. His values have been thrown overboard. We have redefined ourselves to suggest that God has usurped our strengths. We have calculatedly plotted to dethrone God and have ruled our lives by our standards. Christians have even been shy to mention him in public for fear of offending other people's sensibilities. Sadly we have taken away signs and symbols of his presence from public spaces, crucifixes have been removed from the classroom, and many more. The trust our forefathers had in him has been undermined. Who knows if God left us to the lawlessness of our hearts and allowed us to come to our "senses" and make a return to him as the prodigal son did?

Friends we sing hosanna now, we do so in supplication to God for his merciful intervention in these difficult times we are. We sing hosanna, we do so in faith that our sorrows will turn into joys and our mourning into dancing to the glory of his name. We sing hosanna in faith that all things will be restored in Christ our universal King. We sing hosanna that his peace will rule our hearts and minds and God will be all in all.

My Jesus, as I sing hosanna with the children of Jerusalem, hear my supplication and heal the world, transform the trouble we see today into moments of joy, and unite all things together in your name, for you are the King of kings and the Prince of peace.

MONDAY OF THE HOLY WEEK

John 12:1-11

"Why was this oil not sold for three hundred days' wages and given to the poor?"

When one is busily intending to line one's pocket by plotting the sale of one's own master for 30 pieces of silver, the one will naturally be angered by someone who anoints the same master's feet with oil to the tune of 300 days' wages. Perhaps the one cannot help but hypocritically rationalize and criticize the seeming extravagance in the pious pretense that the oil could have been sold and the proceeds be put into the care of the poor.

Such was the posture of Judas when Jesus visited Bethany before the Passover. Lazarus was present, Martha served the meal and Mary took a liter of costly perfumed oil made from genuine aromatic nard and anointed the feet of Jesus and dried them with her hair. The house was filled with the fragrance of the oil. When Judas complained and pretentiously cited wastage which could have benefited the poor, Jesus replied, "Leave her alone. Let her keep this for the day of my burial. You always have the poor with you, but you do not always have me."

Friends, today's passage allows us to reflect on Judas and Mary.

I see in Judas what prevails in many of us. It is either my way or no other good way. Times are when we are likely to condemn an act, not because it is intrinsically wrong but because it wasn't done the way we would do it. Many a conflict in our homes, in the political arena and the workplace, have their roots in the fact that something was done in a way other than what an opposing party would have chosen. It is an attitude that springs forth from negativity, pessimism, selfishness, and the inability to see any possible good in the other person. If Judas had been a little positive or rather optimistic, he would have noticed just the fragrance of the oil and appreciated the length Mary went to stoop very low to pour honor and worship on Jesus. Scripture has it that perfume and incense bring joy to the heart (Prov. 27:9). See how much joy eluded Judas as a result of his pessimism. Something that should have brought joy to the whole gathering rather brought him a discomfort. In much the same way, our pessimism could cost us the beauty and the joy which the fragrance of Jesus' anointing brings. A pinch of optimism is key to happy living.

Mary of Bethany is a very unique biblical figure. She is noted to have taken a permanent place at the feet of Jesus. She sat at Jesus' feet to listen to His word (Luke 10:39). She fell at Jesus' feet to pour woes (John 11:32). She stooped at Jesus' feet and poured her sweet-scented oil in worship (John 12:3). She is also known as the woman of fragrance. This is because there was a kind of fragrance at every encounter she made with Jesus. In Luke 10, it is a fragrance from food; in John 11, it is a fragrance from the perfumes and spices that masked the stench from death; and in John 12, it is the fragrance from the perfumed oil she poured on Jesus' feet.

In the gospel today, Mary performed a good service for Christ, a service that would never be repeated throughout his earthly life. Hers was a courageous act, a sacrificial one, a self-forgetting act. Christ duly regarded and appreciated her efforts. Different people have different ways of expressing their affection for Jesus and as long as they are authentic in their service to him it does not pay to criticize their genuine and beautiful ways of expressing their love for Christ. In Mary, I see the person who would dare to do what she could; the one who would take the initiative. Mary is that individual who would go the extra mile to demonstrate her love. She is the character that would do an act of devotion the way no one else would. She is that magnanimous being who would give without counting the cost. She did not only dare to dream, neither did she merely entertain some wishful thinking, she defied all odds to do what she deemed fit.

Imagine a Jewish woman who would publicly uncover her hair just to dry and anoint the feet of another person. Hailing from the house of affliction (Bethany), she cared less about any affliction that could come her way for rendering Jesus a loving service in all humility.

Today we are presented with Judas and Mary, respectively, an epitome of avarice and an emblem of kind generosity. Whiles one is characterized by selfishness and pompous greed, the other is characterized by courageous love and selflessness. Whereas one would betray and sell the master for 30 pieces of silver, the other would spend almost 300 days' wages to put fragrance on the master and prepare his body for burial. One looked for what to gain from following Jesus, the other was ready to sacrifice it all for the sake of Jesus. They both made choices, yet one made choices that immortalized him as a traitor, the other immortalized herself as a humble and a loving friend of Jesus whose presence always brought some fragrance into Christ's life.

Day in day out we immortalize ourselves too, what is it that we are etching in the rock of life for ourselves? How would posterity see us when this journey of life is over?

We all make daily choices. We would do well if we stopped every now and then to consider the consequences of our choices and the kind of image they would bring us.

My Jesus, may I choose to position myself constantly at your feet and so taste from the wells of your wisdom that my life would be a sweet fragrance pleasing to you.

Tuesday Of The Holy Week

John 13:21-33, 36-38

"Amen, amen, I say to you, one of you will betray me." "Master, why can I not follow you now? I will lay down my life for you."

One of the most painful experiences a person can make in life is betrayal. It is especially painful when it comes from a trusted fellow.

In my own life, the pain I felt most was the one I suffered from a conspiracy to dent my reputation and to bring my God-given vocation into disrepute. The conspiracy itself was not painful. The false accusations, though potentially damaging, constituted not the pain. Rather, it was the people who orchestrated it. The Psalmist reflects the feeling vividly when he said that if this had been done by an enemy, I could bear his taunts, if a foe had risen against me then I could stand it, but you, my friend, the one with whom I eat bread. Betrayal can be painful but the pain is excruciating when it comes from a trusted one.

Jesus suffered betrayal, he also suffered denial, betrayal from Judas, and denial from Peter. Both were his apostles, his trusted friends. Judas, his financial administrator, and Peter the rock on which he would build his church; they were both his companions. The word companion is very indicative here. It issues forth from the Latin cum and panis, meaning, with and bread. A companion is one with whom I break bread. No wonder Jesus was deeply troubled at the inception of the Last Supper. The one to whom He would hand the morsel after He had dipped it was the one to betray him.

John Crowley makes an interesting distinction between Judas and Peter. According to him, what made Judas' betrayal ugly was that it was premeditated. Whereas Peter denied Jesus out of weakness and cowardice, Judas acted in cold calculating betrayal and greed. Judas' act was a culmination of little willful vices in which he resisted God's grace and blinded himself to his master's kindness. As he pilfered from the apostolic purse, he sold his conscience, his taste for money heightened, his values deteriorated and he was ready and willing to sell Jesus for money. Peter, on the other hand, loved Jesus. His love never waned. Nevertheless, Peter rather acted on emotional impulsive weakness. They both erred. Yet whereas one erred from ill-will with ill-intent, the other erred out of impulse, he acted in his shadows. Perhaps Judas followed Jesus out of enthusiasm whiles Peter did so out of love. Indeed peter himself said, "I will lay down my life for you." Scripture has it that greater love no man has than lay down his life for his friends. So Peter indeed followed Jesus out of love. Enthusiasm, if it does not develop into love, wanes. Love may falter but love never wanes. So whereas Peter could be restored based on love, Judas drove himself to despair and despondency because with the waning of his enthusiasm, he had nothing left in his heart on which to hang. He realized too late that by betraying, he had taken away his power to defend the betrayed and had also robbed the betrayed of his power of self-defense. If he had some love in his heart, perhaps he would have saved himself and seen the master's glorification.

Friends today, the catchword is betrayal. It hurts. It hurts most when it comes from people we trust. It hurts. It hurts both the betrayed and the betrayer. It takes something away from the betrayed but takes everything away from the betrayer. Remember Judas took his life. We are losers if we betray others. A lighted wood never burns another without itself getting burnt into ashes. Never betray and if you are betrayed, think of Jesus, he saw his betrayal as an opportunity to be glorified. In the face of his betrayal, he said, "Now is the Son of Man glorified, and God is glorified in him. If God is glorified in him, God will also glorify him in himself, and he will glorify him at once."

Let us also pay attention to the little sins we commit and sweep under the carpet. They graduate into habits and habits once acquired, become attitudes. When sins become attitudinal they lead to other greater sins. Judas graduated from pilfering to kleptomania. Eventually, he sold his master for peanuts. Let us never ignore our little weaknesses and count them as naughts. They could be indicative of worse habits and attitudes in the offing.

Let us also examine the foundations of our relationships. Love and not enthusiasm should be their driving force. Even if we fall for another out of enthusiasm, let us learn to grow out of it into love. When love falters, enthusiasm will keep us. However, when enthusiasm wanes, there is nothing left to urge us on. Our relationships shatter and good friendships hit the rock when enthusiasm is all we carry with us. Build a relationship on enthusiasm and you will lose all you have built when it wanes, build it on love, and it will stand the test of time. Love conquers all. If we love, we might err on the side of impulse but love will keep us going. If we love, we will never be tempted to err against love willfully and intently, for love conquers every evil.

My Jesus, may I never succumb to the temptation to betray any other. Help me to build my relationships on genuine love and open my eyes to those little weaknesses in me which could easily lead me into mortal sins. I count on you to be my help in all my good intentions.

WEDNESDAY OF THE HOLY WEEK

Matthew 28:14-25

"What are you willing to give me if I hand him over to you?"

Why did Judas betray Jesus? What was his motivation? Some say he did so to push Jesus to display his divine powers. Others suggest he wanted to fast track the establishment of Jesus' kingdom. Some others think he was disgruntled because the leadership of the community of apostles went to someone else. Some think that he was driven by sheer greed. I do not know which opinion is right. However, today's reading gives us an inkling into a probable reason for Judas' betrayal.

He went to the chief priests and said, "What are you willing to give me if I hand him over to you?" The key here is: What will you give me if... All his life, Judas has been motivated by the philosophy whose sole concern is what one will get from any given opportunity. Like the subscribers to this philosophy, his tacit creed had been "What is in it for me?" If he was a thief and pilfered from the apostolic purse, he did so because his sole interest was in what would accrue to him from doing whatever he did. Therefore if anything drove him to betray his master, St. Matthew suggests that it was the spirit of individualism- that philosophy which concerns itself with just the I, me, and myself. I do not think Judas thought for once about whom he was trying to betray at this point.

There could have been a thousand and one reasons for his betrayal but the obvious reason is in "how much will you give me?", in other words, what is in it for me? Whoever is governed by this philosophy is further motivated by greed and selfishness. Such a person is exploitative and manipulative. He acts not out of reason but out of feeling. He does things not because they ought to be done but because it feels good to do them. He further looks forward to doing very little of whatever he does, expecting to make the most out of it. His chief aim is to make a profit even when the profit is not worth it.

Take a close look at Judas. After looking at how much he would get, he took thirty pieces of silver and from then on looked for the opportunity to betray Jesus. What went on in his heart as he waited for the opportune time? If it was not just for the good feeling of doing something for money, what else would be his motivation? Why would he sell his master for a pittance if not for selfishness and greed? And what hard work did he do to even earn the thirty pieces of silver? He issued just a kiss to execute the betrayal. Incidentally, he plotted his master's betrayal and lied about it. When he was confronted with it, far from seeing it as an opportunity for change, he pretentiously denied it: "Surely it is not I, Rabbi?"

Judas reflects the human situation. Quite often, we have all been caught under the web of individualism with its attendant minimalistic hedonism.

How often have I not betrayed Jesus because my primary concern was in what was in it for me? The politician is in public service only to seek what is in it for him. The businessman is in business only to look for what is in it for him. The attorney is handling my case because the stakes are high for him.

How often have I not betrayed Jesus because it felt good to do something contrary to his will? The married man or woman will cheat because it feels good. The accountant will massage the figures because there is pleasure in living big. The teenager will indulge in drugs and promiscuous life because it feels good.

How often have I not betrayed Jesus because I wanted to scratch the surface but make big returns? The student lazied about but expected to make an "A". In our bid to play by these philosophies, we realize they are unsustainable so we resort to systematic lies and deceit to stay our course.

The end result is self-destruction. No wonder Judas committed suicide eventually.

Friends, we can all be victims of individualism. However, Individualism usually begets lies and deceit. Deceit, since it cannot be sustained leads to despair. Despair when it loses hope in God's mercy and forgiveness leads to death- physical and spiritual death. Let us pray in order not to fall prey to the Judas' temptation and ruin our lives in the process.

My Jesus, joy, they say, rests in putting you first, others second and me last. Whenever I am tempted to make myself the center of my choices, may your grace lead me to think of you and seek the common good first so that your own joy will constantly be my strength.

MAUNDY THURSDAY

"He took a towel and tied it around his waist. Then he poured water into a basin and began to wash the disciples' feet and dry them with the towel around his waist."

Pope Emeritus Benedict XVI once said that when power and possessions are seen as ends in themselves, power is used against others, and possessions are used to exclude others. However, anyone who has been given power or possessions must see them as a mandate of service to others.

Once upon a time, I saw a movie about a national leader. Upon his assumption of power, he arrogated to himself the highest honors one could ever think of. He threw his weight about, showing a lack of charity to the foreigner and lording it over the citizen. His word was his bond and no one dared to challenge his judgments. His excesses were unimaginable. He was an embodiment of disrespect to all world leaders and used his power to exclude all he deemed were below his dignity. He dealt mercilessly with his perceived enemies and chased out those he considered parasites. I do not know if the movie was a true representation of this so-called leader but it succeeded in painting the picture of what it means to see power as an end in itself and not a means to an end, power not as a call to service but empowerment to bullying.

Jesus Christ is the Son of God. At his name, every knee should bend and every tongue should confess that he is the King of glory. To him was given all the powers in heaven, on earth, and under the earth. He himself asserted that every power and all authority in heaven and on earth had been given to him. It is in that power that he commissioned his apostles to go make disciples of the nations. Today we see him on his knees at the feet of his apostles to wash their feet and dry them. He washes their feet. He does a servant's job. He does something menial. He does it to demonstrate his love. On his knees at the feet of the apostles, he gives a special image to our God. Our God is the power and authority who stoops in humility to raise us up. He does so even when we know we do not deserve his honors. Peter had to protest because it was too much for him to bear. He did not deserve to be washed by Jesus. Yet Jesus insists on washing him, else he would have no part in Jesus. In this act of Jesus, our "God who is absolute power itself, doesn't want to trample on us, but kneels down before us so as to exalt us." (Benedict). It is in his ability to take the form of a servant that we see God's greatness. As the Pontiff would say, "God does not always need to take the highest place." It is in his taking the lowest place that he manifests his power and his love. To save us, he emptied himself and became like us in all things, not counting equality with God something to grasp.

Friends, power struggle is the order of our times. If there is a canker that is eating up the fiber of our society, it has its roots in power struggle. I dare to say that a critical look into the origins of the present pandemic (CoViD-19) would surely point to the same direction-the struggle for power and prominence. It rears its head in the global order, in the family, at the workplace, in the church's hierarchy, and her rank and file, among colleagues and friends, and many more. We are ready to kill and destroy just to have a taste of power and if we cannot have it, all potential leaders must be thrown under the bus. Fraternities have been destroyed and trusts betrayed all in the ambition to winning power and being great. Yet what is power, what is greatness, if it is not to get us on our knees to raise others up? This is what Jesus did. He went down his knees to take away the scales of dust that had gathered on the feet of the apostles and make them worthy to share in the Eucharist. He did what none was ready to do so that they would be worthy to sit at table with him.

Power, they say corrupts; and absolute power corrupts absolutely. However, power corrupts only when our understanding of it is warped. Today, Jesus gives us a new definition of power. He charges us to do exactly as he has done as our Lord and master. If all of us would begin to redefine our sense of power and authority, seeing them as a mandate to serve and not a call to fill the front pages and the headlines, if all of us would view power as a mandate to serve and transform lives, if we would but see power, not as a means to further ourselves, some of the troubles we see now would be no more and peace will prevail wherever we find ourselves.

My Jesus, you came in your power to be of service to humanity. Help me to appreciate the share you have given me in your power and put it at the service of my neighbor. May the inordinate desire for power not blind me to my vocation to be love. So that every day, I will live my life in genuine love of you and of my neighbor.

GOOD FRIDAY

"It is finished"

There is no better time to celebrate Good Friday than today. There is no appropriate moment to celebrate the Cross of Jesus other than the times we are in. In this era of CoViD-19, when the whole world is at its wits end in the fight against this deadly virus, nothing brings us more consolation than the Cross of Jesus.

In the paradox of the cross lies human misery. in the processes of the Cross lies the mystery of human aloneness. In the mystery of the Cross is human sin. Yet in that same cross is our hope, consolation, and victory. For weeks, if not months, our world has been in misery, nations have been in total and partial lockdowns and people have felt nothing but alone. Thousands have been infected, many have lost their lives, millions have been bereaved, and uncountable numbers are living in dread. The world today sings nothing but a mournful litany. We have all become men of sorrows. As I write this piece, the voice of my priest friend in NY rings incessantly in my ears, "Joe, my pastor didn't make it. Corona has claimed his life this dawn without any mercy." Sad isn't it? Is there any hope for our world? Will this war ever be won?

The Way of the Cross has always been my favorite Lenten devotion. It always wells in me diverse sentiments. As we go through its motions, we realize man's inhumanity to the God-made-man. This already gives you a premonition into the extent man could go in cruelty against a fellow human being. The passion of Jesus, which we encounter in today's liturgy also reveals to us how the human person can be blinded to the truth if doing so would enable him to have his way. Jesus was innocent, Pilate did not only know it, but he also declared it. However, because human cruelty was at its peak, the truth was shelved so evil would momentarily reign and justice denied. In the end, the abusers had their way. Sinners treated the innocent as sin. The spotless victim was bruised and the savior was wrapped in grief. He was led like a lamb to the slaughter and was executed like a criminal. He who made the world and all that is within it sat on the throne of the cross naked and forlorn. The King of kings wore not a crown of gold but a crown of thorns. He who was like us in all things but sin died not in majesty but a shameful death on the cross. He who knew no sin was given a criminal's death sentence. He cried, "It is finished". Darkness covered the world and for a moment, evil seemed to have conquered the good. For a moment darkness seemed to have won the day. For a moment the executioners seemed to have won the battle. Yet the victory belonged to Christ. In his cross, love and mercy found me. In his blood, my sin and weaknesses were cleansed. In the shadows of the Cross, the bright and Morning star shed its beams around me. Cantalamessa, states it beautifully that, His cross is the living proclamation that the final victory does not belong to the one who triumphs over others but to the one who triumphs over self; not to the one who causes suffering but to the one who is suffering.

This is where we find consolation in the cross. Jesus on the cross is like the world threatened by a pandemic. All of us, the infected, the yet to be, the dying, the dead, the bereaved, and all who live in perpetual dread of this virus can identify with the crucified Jesus. Ours was the suffering he bore. By his death on the cross, he nailed our deaths, sufferings, and anxieties to the cross so that in his cross we are liberated and won back to God. Through his suffering, we are redeemed. Human ambitions and selfishness could bring us pain and suffering but if our suffering today is united to that of Jesus on the cross, we will realize too soon that victory is not for the aggressor, victory is not for the perpetrator of evil, victory is not for the efficient cause of suffering but rather for the one who suffers in faith and in union with the Son of God who died on the cross to save us.

Friends, today, our fears are real and our anxieties palpable; let us lay our troubles on his shoulders, and put our worries in his pocket, let us unite with him in his passion and go the way of the Cross with him. In his victory on the cross, we shall find not only our victory over a pandemic but also our redemption and our salvation.

We adore you oh Christ and we honor you. Because by your holy Cross you have redeemed the world.

EASTER SEASON

Easter Monday

Matthew 28:8-15

"...then they gave a large sum of money to the soldiers,
telling them, "You are to say, 'His disciples came
by night and stole him while we were asleep.'"

On Good Friday, Pilate asked Jesus, "What is Truth?" He received no answer because an answer from Jesus would have been tautologous, a truism. Jesus is the truth. He was sent because of the truth. He came into the world because of the truth. He came to testify to the truth. Those who belong to the truth belong to him. No one beholds the truth par excellence and demands what truth is. Truth is one, it is simple and is devoid of duplicity. Truth is immutable, it is unchangeable, it is unalterable. Truth is eternal, it is everlasting. It is what it is as it was and it will be forever. Truth stands. The Akans in Ghana say that the truth is like smoke. One may strive to stifle it but it will always come out. Truth can never be covered. No wonder Mary Magdalene and the other Mary met the gravestone rolled and Jesus, risen as he said. The Resurrection of Jesus is one big truth and as the Truth, it is true even when people refuse to accept it. It does not need people's beliefs and acceptance to be true. It is for this reason why St. Paul opined that our faith would have been in vain if Christ had not risen. That he has risen, cannot be denied, neither can the storyline be changed.

Today, the Chief priests and the elders are trying to circumvent the reality of the Resurrection. They take counsel and bribe the soldiers to lie about it, claiming the disciples made away with Jesus' body whiles the soldiers slept on duty. They even assure the soldiers of protection in the sight of the Governor just to get them to lie about the Resurrection. To this day, we are told that this is the story that has circulated among the Jews. What is the story? I do not think it is the story that Jesus' body was stolen but the story that the chief priests and the Pharisees dishonestly tried to make falsehood out of the truth. What prevailed was the truth and the truth is that Christ has indeed risen. He has risen as he said. And we who have died and have risen with him sing Alleluia because death could not prevail over him and that we have life because he lives.

Friends, sometimes human conduct makes the belief that truth no longer exists. In many circles, people promote falsehood and tend to prefer falsehood to the truth. People lie and courageously defend their lies as truth. In their bid to protect or promote their selfish interests, people concoct gullible stories, resort to forgeries, and manufacture fake ideas and throw them in the faces of others. Some people have lied so much in their lives that their very existence and being are synonymous with falsehood. Behold them and you will see falsehood personified. In the family, husband and wife lie to each other without qualms, children have learned from parents to lie and have overtaken their parents in the art of lying. The student is cheating in the exam to make a decent grade. Employees are cutting corners to earn big and employers are not telling them the whole truth. Traders deceive unsuspecting clients and businessmen and women lie about their goods and services. Turn on the radio or the TV today and you will realize how different media houses project the truth to suit their bidding. Different political dispensations make the matter worse. Each accuses the other of falsehood and in the bid to win the next elections, they feed the electorates with false information and vilify one another. The truth has therefore been shrouded in the dark and people can hardly tell the truth from falsehood. People under oath lie between their teeth without qualms and the innocent are counted guilty because we prefer believing in palatable lies to accepting the bitter truth.

If we are an Easter people, we are reminded that one of the early blows to the resurrection story was a plot to make its inherent truth null and void. Soldiers were paid to lie about it. But since the truth cannot be buried,

Jesus indeed rose from the dead, the stone was rolled away and the truth of his resurrection still stands. We who are a people of the resurrection are therefore called to a life of truth, and it will be sane to stand by the truth, live by the truth, die for the truth, witness to the truth, speak the truth and live the truth every day of our lives.

My Jesus, you are the way, the truth, and the life. Grant me the grace to walk in your truth so that I may have a share in the life for which your blood was poured on Calvary.

EASTER TUESDAY

John 20:11-18

Jesus said to her, "Mary!"

For the first time in my life, I have struggled to find something to say in answer to the question: How was your Easter? As a matter of fact, if many of us are better off than Mary Magdalene, we are only so because Easter Sunday did not find us at the grave of Jesus in tears. Like her, the day of the Resurrection found many of us in a pretty sad mood, if not weeping. For some of us, our tears became our bread. For many others, try as they would, the joy of Easter simply eluded them and the tears of CoViD-19 and the consequent lock downs blinded them to seeing the Risen Lord. Even when they saw him, they took him for a gardener, someone other than who he truly is. That notwithstanding, the resurrection experience reminds us of three important things that should always make us joyful: He knows our names. He calls us brothers (and sisters). His Father is our Father and his God our God.

Today, Mary Magdalene goes to the tomb. Even in the sight of two angels, she still entertains the belief that Jesus' body has been taken away. She continues to weep to the extent that when Jesus made an appearance, she couldn't make him out. Her tears had so blinded her that she mistook Jesus for a gardener. What marvels me here is that even in her perplexity she still remains as courteous as would refer to the so-called gardener as Sir. I am also touched by her courage to demand where Jesus' body was and her confidence that she had enough energy to singlehandedly go get it. They who out of love seek Jesus even in desperate situations would surely find him and their tears would be turned into dancing. So Jesus transforms the atmosphere by calling her by name: Mary. At the mention of her name, Mary had a new understanding, the scales of tears fell off her eyes, her perception of Jesus transformed from a gardener to Rabbuoni, teacher. For in that brief experience, Jesus had not only taught her that he was alive but also that he knows her by name. Overjoyed, she began clinging to Jesus like a leech. Jesus knowing that she had a bigger mission than clinging to him, rather made her an apostle to proclaim the Resurrection to his brothers

Friends, in the Bible, to know one's name is very significant. It is like having a certain authority or leverage on that person. McRaes vividly suggests that He who knows my name is my Maker. He formed my heart even before time began and my life is in his hands. He does not only know my name, but he also knows my thoughts, he sees my every tear and he makes himself available when I seek him. He hears me when I call. This is how I see Mary's experience on the day of the Resurrection. Like Mary, Jesus knows my name. He knows your name. He knows our names. He has everything that concerns us under his control. There is no trouble we see that he cannot transform into gladness. The resurrection should, therefore, shake us up from the pain and the burden of CoViD-19, knowing that he who is risen knows our names.

Jesus also said to Mary: "'go to my brothers and tell them, 'I am going to my Father and your Father, to my God and your God.'"

All this while Jesus' disciples had been referred to as servants and friends. By the power of the resurrection, they had been transformed into brothers and sisters of Jesus. That had been elevated to the level of fellows from the same womb (cf the Greek adelphos- brother, adelphe-sister, delphe-womb). This reality of the resurrection must also bring us joy. Joy because Jesus makes us one in him. He unites in himself as siblings from the same womb and makes us children of God. In the Risen Jesus, we can dare to call God, Abba! And so he is not afraid to call God his father and our father; God, his God, and our God.

So to the question: How was my Easter? I would say, Not as it has always been by way of celebration but it has been as good as has brought a reassurance that He knows me by name, that He calls me brother/sister, that He is my God and my Father. These are the thoughts that make me sing Hallelujah even in the midst of a pandemic.

My Risen Jesus, you know me by name and have got the whole world in your hands. When the eventualities of life bog me down may the joys and the promises of the resurrection abound to balance my affliction.

EASTER WEDNESDAY

Luke 24:13-35

"That very day, the first day of the week, two
of Jesus' disciples were going to a village seven
miles from Jerusalem called Emmaus,"

How do we handle disappointments? There are people who have the
ability to take in disappointments with stoic calmness; others do so
with all the clamorous aggression the world can find. Some people meet
disappointments and their world comes to an end, others suffer them and
plunge themselves into despair and depression. Others do so and life is
never the same anymore. Yet disappointments in life are unavoidable. In
Charles Dickens' Great Expectations, Miss Havisham, a wealthy spinster
who was jilted at the altar on her wedding day, locked herself up, donned
her wedding dress and had her wedding cake displayed for the rest of her
life. She could never overcome the consequent shock and trauma that
ensued her disappointment. In as long as we have expectations we shall
have disappointments too. This is because not all our expectations will
always be met and in the manner we anticipate them to be.

The story of the Emmaus journey is basically one of disappointment. On
the day of the Resurrection, two of Jesus' disciples, Cleopas and another,
walked from Jerusalem to Emmaus. They conversed as they went along.
A stranger joined them and inquired as to what it was they talked about.
They marveled at his ignorance and queried if he was the only stranger in
Jerusalem, not knowing the story of Jesus' crucifixion. They then expressed

their disappointment: But we were hoping that he would be the one to redeem Israel. They had hope. Their hope was apparently not fulfilled so they walked away. As they expressed their disappointment and the gullible stories of the women and some apostles, Jesus rebuked their folly for not believing in the prophets. He then broke the Word to them beginning from Moses and the prophets. As they were nearing their destination, they begged him to stay with them for it was dark. while he was with them at table, he took bread, said the blessing, broke it, and gave it to them. With that, their eyes were opened and they recognized him, but he vanished from their sight. They hastened back to Jerusalem to join the others and tell their story.

Friends, the key to this passage William Barclay sets in the Geographical locations of Jerusalem and Emmaus. Emmaus, which means warmth, was to the west of Jerusalem. These disciples who traveled to Emmaus technically journeyed to the west. A journey to the West as against the East is a journey towards the sunset. Think of the Patriarch Abraham. Every journey he made was to the east. The only time he went to the west, he went to Bethel which means God's house. The people of Israel in the desert also journeyed to the east, they journeyed towards sunrise. Sunset depicts darkness. Darkness depicts, evil, sin, depravity, negativity, etc. Cleopas and his unnamed companion in their disappointment journeyed to Emmaus. So in disappointment, they tried to seek consolation in the sunset and comfort in the darkness. What saved them was Jesus' real presence, the Word he shared and the bread he blessed and broke.

Today, we encounter a bunch of disappointed disciples who break away from the company of apostles. They look for an escape in Emmaus. In doing so they step into the darkness. Only God knows what would have happened to them in their sojourn in Emmaus. Jesus' intervention returns them to sunrise and light.

We are not immune to disappointments. When we are, what do we do? Walk away? Where do we go? Into the dungeons? Where is my own Emmaus when I am disappointed? Where do I take consolation in my trying times? Do I launch into self-destruction when I am disappointed? Do I journey towards sunrise or I journey towards sunset?

Disappointments abound, they are bound to happen. Nevertheless, with Jesus, we shall overcome. In his word, we shall find solace (remember their hearts were burning as Jesus explained the scriptures), and in the breaking of bread, we shall see the light which will direct our feet toward the sunrise. May our disappointments not be sources of destruction but means of finding Jesus and profiting from his word and sacrament.

My Jesus, when my hopes are dashed and my great expectations betrayed, may your Word, your Body, and Blood, and your abiding presence accompany me and direct my feet toward the sunrise.

EASTER THURSDAY

Luke 24:35-48

"Peace be with you."

Pax, Peace! Thumbs up for Jesus. This is a greeting I heard almost every Sunday in the years of my ministry at the University of Ghana Catholic chaplaincy. It is a greeting that lights up the light in the eyes of every catholic student on campus. For some reason, this friend of mine on campus rather preferred to greet me Shalom than Pax. He must have had a reason for his preference. For, if anything at all, Pax is the Latin rendition of the Hebrew Shalom.

So what is Shalom, and what is Pax? They both translate as peace. However, peace in the Hebrew and Aramaic context reflects wholeness, completeness, total wellbeing, a sound mind in a sound body, prosperity. Inherent in it is the essential element of permanence. To wish someone Shalom then is to wish them what life has to be. The situation of Adam and Eve in the Garden of Eden before the Fall is a true reflection of Shalom, a situation where man is not only at peace within himself and with all creation but also at peace with his Creator. The situation where the Creator and the creature freely walk hand in hand in the peace and the cool of the Garden without any thought of concealment.

Pax, on the other hand, is a Roman rendition for Shalom. It basically was used to reflect the cessation of hostilities between the conqueror and the conquered; the absence of strife within the citizenry. Inherent in pax is an element of an end-time as the conqueror could lose power at any given time. The English word peace has its roots in the Latin Pax, Pacis. Peace in English is thus close in meaning to the Latin. Often times, it is a treaty that ends a war situation.

Rabbi Khan, therefore, draws a vivid distinction between the two when he opined that while peace can be dictated, Shalom is a mutual agreement. Whiles peace has a temporality to it, Shalom is a permanent agreement. Peace is a treaty to make but Shalom is the condition of peace. There could be negativity in pax, as in the absence of commotion, yet, Shalom, which reflects the presence of serenity, is positive. Finally, as peace is piecemeal, Shalom is whole and complete (see S. Perlman).

On the day of the Resurrection, Jesus appears to the disciples who had locked themselves down for fear of the Jews and perhaps in shame for having failed their master. Contrary to scolding them for their weaknesses he speaks words of peace to them. While they were still speaking about things that had happened, he stood in their midst and said to them, "Peace be with you." As they were startled and troubled, he made a manifestation of his wounds as evidence to the resurrection and topped it with a meal in their sight. He reiterated that all that had been said about him in the Law, the prophets and the Psalms must come true. He opened their minds to understand the Scriptures. He then repeated the prophecy of his passion, death, and resurrection and made them witnesses to the resurrection.

One thing is clear.- that Jesus greeted his disciples with peace. He did it at a time when they were troubled and afraid. He brought them peace when he should have been angry with them. In their time of guilt and trouble was when he spoke Shalom into their lives. A gift of permanent peace. They abandoned him when he was at a point of destruction. He returned their abandonment with total, whole, complete and eternal wellbeing. The bottom line is that Jesus did this when the times were hard and rough for the disciples. They lived in dread of the Jews, they feared they might suffer the same fate he suffered, they were unsure of his own reaction for their denials and betrayal. Their hearts were simply not at peace. Lasting inner peace had eluded them. The Risen Jesus knew exactly what the disciples needed-Shalom, and he gave them exactly that. Having made his own peace available to them, he made them witnesses to the Christ event.

The times are hard. Many of us are troubled and afraid. Like the disciples, we are locked down for the fear of a pandemic. Some of us are doubly locked down because beside the fear of the pandemic, our shortcomings stare us in the face and our consciences won't let us alone in the privacy and the silence of the extended stay at home. We all need peace the way the apostles did. We need genuine peace, peace, not as the world can give, but peace that has an inherent permanence. We need peace that frees the conscience and sets us free. We need positive peace, not merely the absence of wars and pandemics. We need total wellbeing, the sanity of mind, heart and body, internal and external unselfish satisfaction, a condition of strong and unbroken connectedness with God and neighbor, a boundless peace-Shalom, which only the Risen Jesus can give.

May the Risen Lord break into the locked doors of our hearts and homes today and repeat his resurrection greeting of true and abiding peace to us all-Shalom!

Lord Jesus, you gave peace to your apostles and left them with your own peace. May that peace reign and be felt in every heart today, especially those that are troubled by the terror and the scare of this pandemic.

EASTER FRIDAY

John 21:1-14

"So the disciple whom Jesus loved said to Peter, "It is the Lord.""

Love, they say, inspires the heart. It puts a new song into the heart, a song that can be appreciated by the heart alone. Love is also an inspiration to the lips. A person in love easily speaks fondly of their love. Love also inspires the mind. It is obviously very hard for people genuinely in love to obliterate each other from their minds. Where love abounds, the heart's desires, the mind's thoughts, and the words of the lips are essentially about the object of love. Love definitely has a tremendous impact on human elements. One important element on which love impacts without measure is the human eye. For this reason, the early Romans had an adage that says, "Ubi amor est, ibi oculus est". This literally translates as where there is love, there is sight. In other words, love begets sight.

Reflecting on Jesus' Resurrection appearances, Pope Emeritus Benedict XVI, asked a very interesting question. Why did the Risen Lord not go in triumph to the Pharisees and Pilate to show them that he was alive and to let them touch his scars? In response to this question, the Pontiff made the following interventions:

a. The Risen One can not be seen as a piece of wood or stone.

b. The Risen One can only be seen by the person to whom he reveals himself.

c. The Risen One only reveals himself to the person to whom he can entrust with a mission.

d. The Risen One does not reveal himself to curiosity but to love. According to him, love is the only indispensable organ if we are to see and apprehend the Risen Jesus. I think the reverse is true that hatred and hard-heartedness have no eye to see and apprehend the Risen One. If I hate or dislike someone, hardly will I have the eye to see the person, let alone apprehend and appreciate the good in them and all they stand for.

Today, we encounter another episode of Jesus' Resurrection-appearances to the apostles. For the third time, he reveals himself to them. This time around to seven of them by the Sea of Tiberias. Simon Peter decides to go back to his former trade and he is joined by six others. They toil all night but to no avail. While it was still dark they obey a stranger at the shore who guides them to cast their net to the right side of the boat. They catch as many and big fish (153 fish) as they could not haul ashore. So the disciple whom Jesus loved said to Peter, "It is the Lord." When Simon Peter heard that it was the Lord, he tucked in his garment, for he was lightly clad, and jumped into the sea. At the shore, is a charcoal fire with fish on it. Jesus demands they bring some of the fish they just had. Peter singlehandedly hauls the net and brings in some fish to be roasted. At breakfast with him, Jesus gives them bread and fish and none dares to ask of his identity because they know he is the Lord.

Friends, what strikes me in this gospel is that even though Jesus had made earlier appearances to the apostles, they still failed to recognize him. It took the Beloved Disciple to make him out and proclaim that it is the Lord. Where there is love there is an eye. Only love can generate an eye that can see and apprehend God. Only love can beget the sight that will spot and appreciate the good in another person even through the darkness of the dawn. When love is stifled, eyes are no eyes, and they are blinded to seeing God, his image and likeness in humanity, and the good in all his creation.

Have you ever encountered married persons complain bitterly about their spouses? Have you seen priests at war with their bishops before? Have you seen employees dissect their employers? Have you ever experienced politicians and citizens malign the head of state? Have you paid attention to stepchildren fuming with bitterness against their parents? Have you witnessed a rancorous sibling rivalry before? Think of the teacher you never ever complimented. One may ask, what is the source of all these? Is it not the diminution or the absence of love in our hearts that blinds us to the Good in others. Take time to examine the real reason why you're excessively critical of another person and you will realize that you haven't really got love enough in your heart for that fellow. When love is lacking, we fail to see others, let alone appreciate what they stand for and the effort they put into life. We destroy ourselves, one another, and our world if we fail to give love a chance. This is because without love we have no eyes to see each other's worth. If John recognized the Risen One, it is because he had a heart full of love for Jesus. If we ourselves will see Jesus, we shall do so because we have hearts akin to John's. And a heart that has love enough to recognize Jesus will be disposed to love and recognize the good even in the worst person the world could ever find. No wonder the greatest advice John the beloved disciple gave was to ask us to love. Beloved, let us, love, for in the fullness of love we develop the sight to see Jesus as he really is and one another as God made us.

My Jesus, love was the foundation of your resurrection appearances and to those who loved, you also gave sight to see you as you are. Increase the love in my heart, so I may have the strength of sight to see you clearly and love you in my neighbor.

EASTER SATURDAY

Mark 16:9-15

"Go into the whole world and proclaim
the Gospel to every creature."

The Prophet Isaiah paints a very high image of God, as against man, when he depicts God as saying, "My thoughts are not your thoughts...neither are my ways your ways. As high as the heavens are above the earth, so are my ways above your ways and my thoughts above your thoughts." Certainly, God is not like us. If he were, he would have conducted his affairs just the way we would. The Akans of Ghana say that it is the prudent and the wise who is sent on errands but not the long-legged. I dare say that God would do just the opposite. He has the ability to entrust his graces to the foolish in the sight of the world and engages them the way the world would not. Our world would hardly give a chance to him who has blown it but God in his kindness always gives us the chance, even when we are undeserving of it.

Today, we read a section of the longer ending of St. Mark. In this pericope, the biblical writer eclectically attempts a summary of Jesus' resurrection appearances. He appeared to Mary Magdalene from whom he expelled seven demons, he also appeared to the two on their way to Emmaus. They all recounted their experiences but the apostles failed to believe. He later appeared to the eleven while they were at table. He rebuked them for their unbelief and hardheartedness. Notwithstanding the rebuke, he gave them the great commissioning: "Go into the whole world and proclaim the Gospel to every creature."

Friends, I am wondering what kind of businessman would entrust his fortunes to people who do not believe and have hardened their hearts to his vision. Who would ever send a person who has betrayed, denied, abandoned, and manifestly expressed unbelief in the very foundation of his mission in life? Yet because Jesus is God and his ways and thoughts are not ours, he does exactly so. By all standards, these disciples (at least some) had proven themselves unreliable, and yet they are the very ones Jesus engages. How can his ways and thoughts not be above ours?

Jesus upbraids them for their unbelief, yet he does not condemn them to hell. He rather entrusts them with his word and commissions them to evangelize. What a risk Jesus takes! He risks entrusting the perpetration of his kingdom to a bunch of unbelieving, obstinate apostles. He does this as if to say that the power to do his will does not depend on us. St Paul was not a believer when he was called. In fact, he was en route to persecute the church when he met his conversion. He who was once imprisoning the mystical body of Christ later became a prisoner for Christ and he had no qualms affirming that we carry the graces of God in earthenware vessels. None of us deserves to be an instrument in God's hands. None of us is worthy enough to stand in God's sight. If we are, it is because of his own initiative; if we are it is because he is ready to take risks with us. If we are, it is because God is free to do what he wants with whatever he's got. God is ready to use what would ordinarily be counted as naughts to accomplish his designs. He uses the weak to shame the strong. This calls us to humility and a life of total dependence on him. Because He calls us not because we deserved to be called, he calls us not because we are worthy, he calls us because God chooses to. He calls us because he is kind and his kindness overcomes our weaknesses, his kindness covers our unbelief, his kindness cancels our sins, his kindness accords us his blessings, and his kindness makes us worthy of him.

With us, God continues in his risk-taking business. Despite ourselves and while we remain in selfishness, unbelief, and sin, he continues to show us his kindness. Let us drink from the wellsprings of his kindness and learn to be equally kind to others even when they do not deserve our kindness.

My Jesus, you commissioned your apostles to propagate your kingdom despite their limitations. Kindly fill the emptiness of my earthenware vessel and use me despite my excesses to bring your love and salvation to others.

SECOND SUNDAY OF EASTER

John 20:19-31

Peace is His Gift

"Jesus came and stood in their midst and said to
them, "Peace be with you." When he had said this,
he showed them his hands and his side."

A story is told of a young seminarian named Benjamin who paid a visit to
a retired priest living in a nursing home. Fr. John, who was in his 90's had
served as a pastor in several churches throughout his diocese. As soon as
Benjamin asked for Fr John, the nurse at the desk perked up considerably.
She offered to show him to Fr John's room herself. On the way, she
described how the elderly priest was an encouragement for the entire staff
and the other patients. She said he was the most active retired person she
had ever met. He had started a whole series of activities in the nursing
home, despite the constant pain his illnesses were causing him. With that,
they reached the end of the hallway and the nurse introduced Benjamin
to Fr John. At the end of their nearly two hours encounter, Benjamin
penned down his impression of Fr. John: "During our conversation, I was
deeply inspired by his wisdom and accomplishments. However, I think I
was even more impressed by his contagious joy and simplicity, and more
importantly, by the peace, his presence exuded. It was easy to understand
why everyone admired him so much."

Where had Fr John learned his wisdom? What was the secret to his joy? What was the source of the peace that flowed from his heart despite his pain? As visiting hours came to an end, one of the nurses popped her head into the doorway to ask Fr. John if he had taken his medicine. The ever pleasant old priest smiled, pointed towards the wall, and responded, "Thank you, but my medicine is over there." Curious, the nurse looked around the door to see what he was pointing at. It was a crucifix (See ePriest).

Friends, whenever the word peace is mentioned, our thoughts immediately go to the absence of conflict, the presence of quiet and rest, everyone agreeing and getting along. For many of us, peace is synonymous with tranquility, absence of war, stillness, and trouble-free nonviolent life conditions.

In the Gospel of St. John (20:19-30), the Risen Jesus' greeting to his disciples was "Peace be with you." Twice on his first appearance to them when Thomas was absent, and a third time when he appeared to them again the following week. What did Jesus have in mind when he greeted them with peace? We all know that peace, the kind the world knows is more of complacency than peace. It is man's self-satisfaction that is usually devoid of one's awareness of actual dangers or deficiencies. It is that self-satisfied peace that lures man to sleep and has the potential of leading him to the loss of the most valuable things in life.

What Jesus had in mind when he offered his disciples peace thus comes clear when put into its proper context. As Jesus declares peace to his disciples, one of the first things he does is to impress upon them the wounds of his crucifixion. We are told in Scripture that when he had said this, he showed them his hands and his side. He also announces his intention to send them in the same way that he himself was sent by his Father. In his words, "As the Father has sent me, so I send you." He then gives them the gift of the Holy Spirit with the power to forgive sins. Taken together, we can conclude that the peace Jesus offers has more to do than ensure tranquility, harmony, and affability. Jesus invites his disciples into the same activity of peacemaking that characterized his own life and mission, the same activity that led him to the cross. Fr. John had learned his lines well when he saw his medicines in the cross on the wall. He knew quite well that price of peace, of interior harmony and strength, is in the Passion - Christ's Passion, and our own passions, united to his.

Certainly, God the Father did not send the Son into the world merely to bring tranquility, harmony, and affability. Jesus worked for peace by bringing back into the fold the outcast and the marginalized. He sought to turn upside down the societal conventions of first and last, blessed and cursed, rich and poor. His peace invited the lion to see the lamb as neighbor and friend, the Jew to speak with the Samaritan, and the prostitute to dine with the Pharisee. Jesus' offer of peace to the world was, therefore, an offer of a radically new way of being in the world. Such was the mission he entrusted to the disciples when he offered them his peace, showed them his wounds, and gave them his breath of new life with the mandate to forgive sins. That offer he made at the Resurrection appearances he makes to us today, and he sends us just as the Father sent him. We are to be peacemakers just as Jesus was and the Cross must be the price we pay for the peace we make (see K. J. Largen).

We live in a world marred by war in every corner. Society today incarcerates a vast number of men and women and then forgets about them. Many a country is replete with guns without effective gun control laws and too many children's lives are marred by violence at home, at school, and at play. Countries around the world continue to live in dread of rogue States who pose a perpetual threat by the clandestine gathering of weapons of mass destruction. In a world where terrorists have no qualms bombing masses of innocent people in God's own house, where someone's mischief or deliberate error can cause a pandemic to exterminate whole populations, and many more unsightly vicious eventualities occur, ours is the vocation to follow Jesus in his radical peacemaking venture. We have the mandate to heal the world and make it a better place for all. We have the vocation to offer and foster unconditional forgiveness, the kind that would bring about and maintain the Kingdom of God in the here and now. In the power of the Holy Spirit and in the spirit of the Cross which was the price he himself paid for launching peace, and in trusting that Christ himself continues to work in us, may we all continue to provide leaven to our needy society and transform it persistently until the day when Christ will come again to perfect his work and inaugurate the fullness of his peace (see Largen).

Have a peaceful week.

MONDAY OF THE SECOND WEEK OF EASTER

John 3:1-8

"Amen, amen, I say to you, unless one is born from above, he cannot see the Kingdom of God."

The story of Jesus' encounter with Nicodemus is well known in many Christian circles. Scholars are of the view that one of the gifts and burdens of the story is its familiarity. I was a young seminarian on vacation when a gentleman I met in town one day decided to engage me in a conversation. Bible in had and assuming every air of superiority, he inquired about my religious affiliation. When I told him I was catholic, his next question was: Are you born again? Anticipating where the conversation would lead us both, I simply said no. How I wished I had said yes! From that day on, this gentleman would never smile at me nor respond to my greeting whenever our paths crossed. E. Searcy was right when he opined that many people consider the words "born again" as a slogan, a badge of honor, a tool to distinguish insider from an outsider, and saved from lost. Christian homes have been divided because of differing convictions regarding what it means to be born again. What therefore is our take in this whole passage?

Nicodemus was a Pharisee, a member of the Sanhedrin and for that matter a ruler the Jews. Impressed by the signs Jesus worked and convinced that no such signs could come from anyone except by the power of God, he made a nightly visit to Jesus. He acknowledged Jesus as Rabbi, a teacher who had come from God, and affirmed all Jesus' signs proved that God was with him. Without waiting for any further appellations, Jesus made a statement that has become famous among Christians: "Amen, amen, I say to you, unless one is born again, he cannot see the Kingdom of God." Obviously, Nicodemus and Jesus were on different wavelengths. The Greek term Jesus used was Anōthen. Anōthen means one of two things: "again" or "from above". Nicodemus took Jesus to be saying unless one is born again. He, therefore, queried as to how an adult could reenter the mother's womb and become a neonate. Jesus clarifies his position by saying, "Amen, amen, I say to you, unless one is born of water and Spirit he cannot enter the Kingdom of God.

In this clarification, Jesus does a number of things:

1. He makes a paradigm shift from "seeing the kingdom" to "entering the kingdom".
2. He distinguishes between being born again as in the flesh and being born from above.
3. He further explains birth from above to be constituted in water and the Holy Spirit.

For Jesus, therefore, to be born again is not necessarily fleshly. It is rather a birth from above. It is a birth that does not depend solely on human effort but on water and the Spirit. If water is the symbolism of baptism and baptism is a sacrament, then being born of water is an outward sign of inward grace. The outward dimension is accomplished through human action. However, the inward grace is an act of God, an act of the Spirit, an enactable solely by the Spirit. To be born again, therefore, is not to be determined by man. This is because the ultimate determinant of heavenly rebirth is like the wind that blows where She wills, whence She wills, and gives cleansing to whomever She pleases. As Jesus himself continued to say, "What is born of the flesh is flesh and what is born of spirit is spirit... The wind blows where it wills, and you can hear the sound it makes, but you do not know where it comes from or where it goes; so it is with everyone who is born of the Spirit." To be born again, therefore, is to be born of God, to be born of the Spirit. It is God who gives us new birth in Christ Jesus and the Spirit He has sent.

Friends, today permit me to underscore a number of things. Jesus' paradigm shift from seeing the kingdom to entering the kingdom suggests that there is one thing to see what is needed and there is another thing doing it. How often do we see the way of Jesus? We hear his command to forgive. We are drawn to his walk with the poor, the outcast, the marginalized. Yet, we hold on to our old habits, family patterns, and cultural norms which are beyond our power to break and change. As Searcy would put it, "We see but cannot dare to enter the new world that is the kingdom of God." Let us strive to move from merely seeing God's Kingdom to entering it. Let us not merely see the sight and talk the talk, let us also walk the sight and the talk. Our faith must not only be in seeing it must also be in entering the Kingdom.

To be born again, we need to be born of water and the Spirit. Our human and religious traditions cannot stifle the free flow of the Spirit. We cannot, therefore, use our "born again" jargons and badges to judge and condemn others, looking down on them as if the power of rebirth depends on us. Later on, Jesus would say, It is the spirit that gives life, the flesh is of no avail; the words that I have spoken to you are spirit and life."

Nicodemus was an accomplished Jew, a learned man, a man of knowledge and wisdom, a man known to have had an impressive set of institutional credentials, all the same, something was lacking in him; an emptiness which only Jesus could fill. We could be as good as he is, but something would still be missing. It should not be too difficult for us to make a return to Jesus, even if necodemously, to seek his help and ask him to fill that vacuum in our lives. B. Younger drives home this thought when he said that life is a mystery beyond our understanding, a gift that only God can give. Any life we know comes as a gift of God. Hope and joy come from God. The same Spirit who gave life in the first place gives life over and over again. Our life, therefore, would be meaningful only if we lay it bare for Christ to fill its empty spaces.

My Jesus, I come to you with my inadequacies which you alone can fill. May your Spirit blow into my life and create me anew so that all that I have and are will be seeds to be sown today for the eternal harvest.

TUESDAY OF THE SECOND WEEK OF EASTER

John. 3:7b-15

"And just as Moses lifted up the serpent in the desert,
so must the Son of Man be lifted up, so that everyone
who believes in him may have eternal life."

Sometimes life throws stones at us. Other times our choices attract calamities and misfortunes our way. Yet other times other people's conduct puts us in harm's way. When Moses mounted the Bronze Serpent in the desert, the people of Israel had demonstrated gross ingratitude to Yahweh and His servant after all the initiatives God had put in place to liberate them from slavery in Egypt. They whined, the complained, they tried and tested the same God whose hands carried them through the Red Sea to safety in the desert. Their continued attachment to things of Egypt, their prejudices, idolatry, and weaknesses broke down their defense in God. They made choices, choices which landed them in a colony of venomous serpents whose fangs meted out death to them on account of their sins. Moses' Bronze Serpent served to save them from death.

In his encounter with Nicodemus, Jesus alludes to the Bronze-serpent effect, saying, "… just as Moses lifted up the serpent in the desert, so must the Son of Man be lifted up, so that everyone who believes in him may have eternal life." Christ on the Cross, Christ who died and rose from the dead is the Saviour of all who look on him and as often as we look upon the Cross when life's challenges and our own willful choices throw stones at us, so often does he forgive us our sins, save us from death and bring us to eternal life.

Nicodemus was struggling. He had a choice to make between keeping his position with the Sanhedrin and accepting Jesus as the Son who alone had been with the Father, had come down from the Father and so could testify to what he knows. Jesus' advice to him was that life could only be found in the Saviour who died on the Cross and rose again and returned to the Father.

Friends, life could beat us too. We might have our own struggles. We could come to the crossroads. Our ill-informed choices could draw a wedge between us and God. We might want to hold on to something earthly which is seemingly promising. Yet, salvation is in Christ; and as often as we look upon Him on the Cross and submit to His holy will, we shall be saved.

My Jesus, in you is my life. When life's choices make me want to cling to worldly pleasures and gains, may your graces turn my gaze to you on the Cross and beyond for salvation.

WEDNESDAY OF THE SECOND WEEK OF EASTER

John 3:16-21

"God so loved the world that he gave his only-begotten Son"

God loves us all. His love knows no boundaries.

God's love is manifested in his giving.

God's love gives God's best- His only begotten Son. In love, God gives his very essence.

God's love is not to condemn us. God's love is to save us.

Salvation is in believing in God and in him whom God has sent.

God's love is light to the world.

We choose to live in the light of his love or to live in darkness.

Living the truth is choosing to live in God's love and light and our deeds will show as being done in God. All the darkness of the world cannot quench even a spark or a ray of God's light. There is thus every good reason not to choose darkness but God's light and so dwell in his love and light up the world.

My God, may you grant us the grace to live in your love today.

THURSDAY OF THE SECOND
WEEK OF EASTER

John 3:31-36

"Whoever accepts his testimony certifies that God is true"

The question of truth has been widely debated in the history of philosophy. Different theories of truth have been propounded, all in the bid to spell out the concept and meaning of truth. Three of these theories have been widely considered. They include the correspondence, the coherence, and the pragmatic theories of truth.

The correspondence theory states that something is true if and only if what it purports tallies with the reality out there. Thus the statement: "It is snowing" is true if and only if out there flakes of snow are falling and there is evidence to that fact. True therefore is what corresponds to reality.

The coherence theorists believe that truth is that which is consistent with a body of beliefs. If I made the statement: " Christians worship the Trinity" and this statement is consistent with Christian beliefs and practices, my statement will be considered as true because of its consistency with what is believed by Christians. True, therefore, is that which coheres with a body of beliefs.

The pragmatic theorists are of the view that truth is workability. Something is true if it is useful. It is true if it works for me and a greater number of people. It is true if it satisfies, it is true if it has utility value, it is true if it brings satisfaction. The idea "God", for instance, is true if it works.

Even though none of these theories individually provides a holistic view of what truth is. They come together to provide a litmus test for truth. Truth, as we know, must be authentic, it must tie in with a system of beliefs and must have a utility value.

To be true, one has to be sincere and not deceitful. A person is true when he has an interest in someone's welfare. He is considered as true because he is firm in allegiance; he is loyal, faithful, and steadfast. A true being is genuine in character. He is undeniable, unvarnished, and real.

In Today's gospel, St. John the Evangelist concludes his third chapter with a complex monologue. It is complex because one can hardly tell who the interlocutor is. Could it be Jesus? He is the one who came from above. Could it be John the Baptist? He is the one who spoke just before this conclusion. Could it be the author himself? The language smacks of his own testimony to Jesus. Nevertheless, the truth of the passage is indisputable. He who is from above is above all. He testifies to heavenly things but no one accepts his testimony. However, those who accept his testimony also certify that God is true. How is God's truth revealed? His truth is revealed in the fact that the one He sent speaks God's word, that he is lavish with the gift of the spirit, that God loves his Son and has handed everything over to him, such that those who believe in him will have life eternal but those who disobey will not see life but have the wrath of God on them.

Friends, central to this gospel is the testimony that God is true, God is trustworthy. By virtue of the Word made Flesh, God expresses his authenticity. He is not a figment of the imagination. God is really real and existentially existent in his Son Jesus Christ. He is the one who has come from above and to have seen him is to have seen the Father. He who has come from above testifies to heavenly things and his testimony is consistent with all that God stands for in his word. If God's Word embodies all that we believe God to be and if all Jesus taught and did point to God, then

Jesus' life and teaching are consistent with the totality of our belief in God. Believing in God has an infinite utility-eternal life. God, therefore, as revealed in Christ Jesus, is all that Truth is- in him resides reality, in him there is consistency and no guile, in him is infinite utility. When Jesus said I am the Way, the Truth, and the Life, he only cemented the fact of the centrality of God's truth and trustworthiness.

We are thus given the chance today to reflect and appreciate our God who is true, authentic, faithful, steadfast, and ready at all moments to give us life in Christ Jesus. If we believe, God is faithful to give us eternal life. It is only our unbelief and disobedience that will call his wrath on ourselves. He is true all the time.

My Jesus, you came to testify to the truth. To those who accept your testimony, you give life eternal. Increase my faith in you and incline my heart to obey your will, that I may never call on God's wrath to befall me.

Friday Of The Second Week Of Easter

John 6:1-15

"Then Jesus took the loaves, gave thanks, and
distributed them to those who were reclining, and
also as much of the fish as they wanted."

The miracle of feeding the multitude was very important to the early Christian community. It was so important that all the evangelists recorded it. In fact, Mark and Matthew did it twice. John's report is rather unique as it mentions certain details that throw special light on the miracle.

According to him, it was around Passover and Jesus went across the Sea of Galilee. He went up the mountain. Crowds who had witnessed his signs he worked for the sick followed him. At the sight of the crowd, he queried Philip as to how food could be procured to feed the crowds. Philip didn't think even eight (six) months' wages would suffice to feed them. Andrew however, though in doubt, presented a lad with five barley loaves and two fish. Jesus took the bread and fish, asked the crowds to be seated on the grass, gave thanks, broke the bread and fish, and distributed them to satisfy the crowd-5000 of them. When the leftovers were gathered, they made twelve wicker baskets full. The people acclaimed Jesus as the expected Prophet but not wanting to be acclaimed a King, Jesus withdrew to the mountain.

As I read this gospel, many sidelights come to the fore. I do not think it was for nothing that the biblical writer indicated the time and place for the miracle. It took place across the Sea of Galilee when the Passover was near. Galilee is in the north and across Galilee is a pagan territory. The Passover is celebrated in the south, in Judah. Why should it be significant to a northern event? Well, some scholars think that it is a subtle way of uniting Jews and Gentiles in the confines of the miracle. Thus, these two details indicate that the miracle reflects the universality of the need which Jesus takes care of. In other words, the mention of Passover and Galilee indicate "a worldwide drama of universal human need and of God's care for that need (Brodie, 1993, see also Feasting on the Gospels). Jesus is capable of meeting the genuine needs of all humanity without any discrimination.

The characters in the passage also cast some light on the miracle. I am wondering why it was Philip that Jesus talks to as to how to obtain food for the crowd and how it happened that it was Andrew who brought the lad to Jesus. The name Philip is revealing. Ordinarily, it means lover of horses. However, if the ultimate letter "P" should count as a variable, then the name could translate as Philia and prosopon. Philia means to love and prosopon means person. Philip would, therefore, mean lover of persons. Andrew ordinarily means manly. To be a man is to be courageous. Andrew thus reflects the quality of courage. One could say then, that, when Jesus asked him who had love in his heart for others a way to take care of a universal human need, courage dared to put what was available into his hands and that universal human need was squarely met. Jesus met the need of the crowd and more.

Friends, we are all instruments in Jesus' hands. If we cultivated genuine love in our hearts for others and embraced the manly virtue of courage, the courage that would dare, despite our doubts, to put our least available resources into his hands, Jesus will graciously take care of every human need and even more.

Let us, therefore, be characterized by love. Love should grant us the courage to bring the little means available to Jesus and see how Jesus will transform our world into a place of peace and tranquility for us all.

My Jesus, incline my heart to the love of others and grant me the courage to bring you the little at hand to be transformed and multiplied to meet every human need.

Saturday of the Second Week of Easter

John 6:16-21

"It is I. Do not be afraid."

Jesus was all night up the hill to pray. He was not at the prayer as if to say his eyes were not his disciples. While at prayer he also watched over them. In the darkness of their life, He knew their plight and came to their aid when the sea was stirred up on account of the strong blowing wind.

Life is a journey. We are all embarked. Sometimes night falls and darkness covers us. Other times the storms rage and we are afraid. But Jesus has his eyes constantly on us. Just as he has his eyes on the sparrow, he watches us too. In his time, he walks through the darkness of our lives, overcomes and calms the storms of the sea of destruction which derails our progress in him and makes us happy again. In our trying moments, let us take time to him say again, "It is I. Do not be afraid."

His ability to commune with the Father and also have his eyes on the needs of his friends is worthy of emulation. For Jesus, time with Father is no time if it does not eventually lead to time in serving the needs of his friends. In just the same way, time with his friends and followers is not time if it does not bring him to solitude with the Father. No wonder after feeding the multitude, Jesus went up the hill to pray and from prayer walked over the sea to allay the fears of his perishing disciples. It is very easy to strike a dichotomy between my spiritual life and my life in community with others and make it seem that the former has absolutely no relation to the latter. Yet, my spirituality is warped if it hangs my feet and prevents them from touching the ground. In much the same way my humanitarian and philanthropic spirit is lopsided if it does not flow from on high and rise up to God like incense. A healthy balance in my spirituality and my love for neighbor must always be maintained. Jesus has shown the way. Ours is to follow.

My Jesus, thank you for constantly fixing your gaze on me and coming to my aid when the storms of life rage and I need you most. May your beneficence be for me an inspiration to be there for all who are in dire need of my sacrificial presence in their lives.

Monday Of The Third Week Of Easter

John 6:22-29

"Do not work for the food that perishes, but for the food that endures for eternal life, which the Son of Man will give you."

Many of the early Christians were fond of the saying: Quid ad aeternitatem? Thus, before they embarked on any action, they would ask whether the said action would serve towards their sanctification and eternal salvation. These would take no action if it does not inure to their eternal inheritance. The idea is that no act is carried out for nothing. There is always a reason in view for doing the things we do. This is not the case only with our day to day endeavors but also in the spiritual realms.

After feeding the multitude and also walking on the sea, Jesus continued to have the crowd on the lookout for him. They put one and two together and figured out that He might have somehow followed his disciples to the west of the sea. They mounted boats and made for Capernaum in search of him. When they found him, they inquired as to when he got there. Jesus avoided their question and pointed out the real reason for their search: Amen, amen, I say to you, you are looking for me not because you saw signs but because you ate the loaves and were filled. Do not work for food that perishes but for the food that endures for eternal life, which the Son of Man will give you. For on him, God, the Father, has set his seal." So they said to him, "What can we do to accomplish the works of God?" Jesus said to them, "This is the work of God, that you believe in the one he sent."

Quite apart from driving home the need to do the right things for the right reasons, I see the biblical writer's genius play on words.

Consider the following: loaves, works of God, work of God. Loaves are synonymous with bread. In the background of the biblical writer, bread is also called "food of the earth" and "work of human hands". So here Jesus seems to have said that you are looking for me because you enjoyed the food of the earth and the works of human hands. Your effort in looking for me is work done in hopes for food of the earth which human hands have made. You should rather labor for food from above which is the work of God's hands. Simply put, seek me not to obtain perishable man-made bread, rather seek me for the Bread that God's hands have made. The crowd got his message right and inquired on how to accomplish the works of God. However, Jesus moves away from "works of God" to "Work of God". For the evangelist, God has one big work, which is in setting his seal on his Son and sending Him so that all who believe in him will have life. To do God's work then is to believe in the one God has sent. He is the Bread of heaven, the bread of life, the food that endures. We may have many toils in life but our preoccupation must ultimately be in seeking the bread which God has made.

Two things are clear, there are the works for loaves, works of human hands, and there is the work of God. The product of the former perishes but that of the latter eternally endures. What then do we work for when we toil daily? Jesus' advice to the crowd is clear: Do not work for the food that perishes, but for the food that endures for eternal life, which the Son of Man will give you.

Friends today, Jesus is not necessarily asking for the neglect of human labor. He is asking us to set our hearts on heavenly things. Consider the jobs and the work that we do to make a living, our striving for power, popularity, pleasure, and possessions, these are never wrong. As a matter of fact, it is right and just to work hard for things that do perish, but that put food on the table and provide security for our families. However, to make these an end in themselves and set our hearts to them, making idols of them without any due regard to God and the eternal life he brings us in

Christ Jesus is the issue. Many a time we miss the mark. We tend to follow God just so his grace will enable us to make ends meet. However, even if God drops manna from on high to fill our physical hunger, his action should point us to eternity but not to leave us in perpetual indulgence in materiality. Our daily toils, even if they begin as works of human hands must eventually lead us to the work of God. For our toils are fruitless if they don't bring us to eternal life.

My Jesus, I believe in you as the Bread that comes down from heaven. Kindly avail yourself to me as my life's companion, so that with you as my guard I will always draw water from the wells of salvation.

TUESDAY OF THE THIRD WEEK OF EASTER

John 6:30-35

"Amen, amen, I say to you, it was not Moses who gave the bread from heaven; my Father gives you the true bread from heaven."

Man is an enigma. He is very hard to understand. Yesterday, the crowd was fed through a miraculous multiplication of a poor boy's bread and fish. As they had their fill and even witnessed twelve wicker baskets full of leftovers, Jesus had to withdraw to the mountain to be alone because they wanted to acclaim him king. The next day, they follow him to Capernaum only to ask him to show them a sign so they would see and believe in him. Before this time, their question to Jesus was, what should we do to accomplish God's works? All they had to do was to believe. Now they shift from what they should do to what Jesus should do to enable them to believe. I am wondering if it was the same crowd Jesus fed that is asking for a sign before they believe. As if asking for a miracle after having been miraculously fed was not enough, they even threw an insinuative challenge at Jesus, "Our ancestors ate the manna in the desert, as it is written: He gave them bread from heaven to eat." They seemed to have forgotten too soon what Jesus could do. They are using their ancestry to transact security for the future. They want to count on grace as mediated by their ancestors. Moses did an act that was favorable to their ancestors at their point of need. Their reliable past must predict their future blessings. Anything short of that will well up no belief in them.

Well, Jesus is always God and God will always be God. He understands the human situation. He thereby anticipates their lack of understanding and straightens their trend of thought. Our ancestral past cannot be a guarantee for future security. So Jesus nicely brings the crowd from the past to the present and points them to the future. It was not Moses who gave the bread from heaven; my Father gives you the true bread from heaven. Mark here that Jesus, while he said it was not Moses who gave…, now says my Father gives. When they politely asked to be given this bread from heaven always, " Jesus said to them, "I am the bread of life; whoever comes to me will never hunger, and whoever believes in me will never thirst." Here, Jesus seems to be saying that the Jews cannot live on borrowed past favors. God's provisions are always available. He gives the Bread from heaven every day. However, the fruits of God's giving accrues only to those who come to him and all who believe in him. They are the ones who will not hunger nor thirst.

Friends, today, the same crowd that witnessed the multiplication of loaves and wanted to make Jesus king asked him for a miracle in order to believe. They are using their ancestral favors as promissory to secure a future for themselves. However, Jesus reminds them that God works a daily miracle of giving them the bread from heaven which is Jesus himself. All they need is to come to Jesus and believe in him, then like their ancestors, they will neither hunger nor thirst.

Sometimes, the human in us rears its head. Like the crowd, we are complex and hard to understand. In one moment we act at our very best. In another moment we are unimaginably at our worst. One would wonder if the Jekyll and Hyde in us constitute the same individual. Yet God understands our human situation. He tolerates our weaknesses and leads us to a better understanding of his ways.

Other times, we are comfortable counting on our ancestral past to transact our salvation in Christ. What we forget is that salvation cannot be borrowed. The fact is that God always makes his Son our Lord Jesus Christ, the Bread of life, available. Our daily coming to him and believing in him is key to our salvation. Rather than seeking miracles and counting on our lucky roots for our salvation, let us come daily to Jesus in his Word and the Sacrament of Bread and Blood to be fed for our eternal salvation.

My Jesus, you are the Bread that the Father sends from heaven. Attract me to your side and incline my will to believe in you so that I will neither be hungry nor thirst anymore.

WEDNESDAY OF THE THIRD WEEK OF EASTER

John 6:35-40

"I will not reject anyone who comes to me."

I once met a lady who looked very depressed and dejected. Undoubtedly, she was beautiful. However, she looked shabby, unkempt, and troubled. The disturbing thing was that she would sometimes walk against oncoming vehicular traffic unawares, lost to herself. After Mass one Sunday, she asked to talk to me because the homily looked like I had her whole life before me like an opened book. As I engaged her in a series of conversations, I grew up to appreciate all the ups and downs she had suffered in life. Simply put, life had beaten her up and had never been kind to her. She had encountered many troubles and had suffered unimaginable calamities in life. As our sessions progressed, I sometimes wondered how she had made it in life until that point. At a time when she had tried all her best to weather the storms of life and made a name for herself was when she met and married the man she thought would make life easier and better. As a matter of fact, she had no one except her husband. She, therefore, pledged her whole life to the success of their union. She went the extra mile to make their marriage work as she made him the center of her life. All was beautiful and well until one day the husband just walked away. Things fell apart and the center could no longer hold for her.

The note he left said he had found a younger and a prettier lady who fulfilled his dreams better and had hooked up with her. He told her she was free to marry any other man of her dreams and wished her the best of luck. A feel of rejection threw this lady into self-pity. Unable to come to terms with all the pains she had suffered, she fell into self-neglect. The sense of rejection succeeded in taking away her interests in life. Joy eluded her, peace was forfeited and one only needed to see her combination of colors for outfits to tell she was a troubled soul. My encounters with her opened my eyes to what it means to feel rejected, abandoned, and the sense of being jilted for another. Thank God she eventually grew past her hurts and found herself back.

Perhaps you have also felt a sense of rejection before. We suffer rejection from friends, parents, children, colleagues, and parishioners. Sometimes we might not be the direct victims of rejection but we may have been acquainted with someone who is. Rejection brings about one thing- it robs its victims of any meaningful life. It actually takes a very strong-willed person to sally through the pain of rejection with ease.

Today Jesus makes a series of statements in response to a crowd that seeks a sign. He is the bread that comes from heaven. Coming to him and believing in him quenches our thirst and satisfies our hunger. He affirms that everything that the Father gives him will come to him and in one of the most consoling statements I find in scripture, he says, "I will not reject anyone who comes to me." His reason for saying this is that he has come from heaven to do the will of the one who sent him. And the will of the one who sent him is summed up as follows: "...that I should not lose anything of what he gave me, but that I should raise it on the last day. For this is the will of my Father, that everyone who sees the Son and believes in him may have eternal life, and I shall raise him on the last day."

Friends, in life, we reject and are rejected. We are witnesses to incidents of rejection and their dire consequences. Human beings fail and reject one another. Jesus never rejects. He is the Bread of life. As Bread Jesus gives us life and sustains our life the way rejections can never destroy. It is his Father's will that Jesus does not only hold us to himself but raise us up and give us life not only in the present but also in eternity. Today's Gospel reading thus gives us an assurance no human can give. Let us hear Jesus' therapeutic words again: I will not reject anyone who comes to me. Even if humans reject us, God never does. We only need to embrace the one He has sent and believe in Him. Then we shall have life here and now and life in eternity.

Give it a second thought whenever you're tempted to reject someone. People are never perfect but rejecting them is never in the will of God. What God accomplishes in Jesus, He does with us too: we shall never reject anyone who comes to us.

My Jesus, you never reject anyone who comes to you, plant in my heart something of your love so that in good times and in bad, I will have the courage to embrace all who come to me as I follow you in doing your Father's will.

THURSDAY OF THE THIRD
WEEK OF EASTER

John 6:44-51

"Your ancestors ate the manna in the desert, but
they died; this is the bread that comes down from
heaven so that one may eat it and not die."

Today we continue reading from the Bread of Life discourse in John 6.
We are precisely reading from verses 44-51. In these verses Jesus says
that whoever listens to the Father and learns from the Father comes to
him, Jesus; and that no one comes to Jesus except the Father draws him.
According to Jesus, the one who came down from God is the only one who
has seen the Father. Whoever believes in Jesus has eternal life. He affirms
himself as the bread of life and tells the crowd that their ancestors ate the
manna in the desert but died. However, He is the bread that comes down
from heaven so that they may eat and not die. Jesus is the living bread that
comes down from heaven. Whoever eats this bread will live forever. The
bread He will give is his flesh for the life of the world.

This pericope is replete with eternal truths. Three times Jesus refers to his
coming: the one who came from God, the bread that came down from
heaven, the living bread that came down from heaven. The repetition must
not be a coincidence. What does it mean for Jesus to leave his glory and
come down from heaven? How did he come down from heaven? When St.
Paul made reference to his coming down, he described him as taking the
form of a servant and being born in human form. He saw in Jesus' coming

down from heaven, an act of humility (Phil 2). Jesus himself describes his coming as in the form of bread, bread which is his flesh to be given for the salvation of the word. Jesus' coming down is therefore seen vividly in the Eucharist. In the Eucharist, God leaves his glory to be with us. The Eucharist thus demonstrates the humility of God who emptied himself for our salvation. For us then, the Eucharist is a way of leaving ourselves behind and entering the life of God. Having been schooled by God from the table of the Word and filled from the table of the Eucharist, we are drawn to an act of self-surrender to the same Jesus who gives us his flesh for our salvation. Pride, therefore, has no place in the one who receives Jesus, the living bread who came down from heaven.

Jesus' words are unequivocal: "I am the living bread that came down from heaven; whoever eats this bread will live forever. " The Eucharist is the pledge of our resurrection. In it, Jesus promises us eternal life. When we eat his body and drink his blood we have eternal life and he will raise us up on the last day.

In the Eucharist, Jesus is really present and he could not have been clearer: "...the bread that I will give is my Flesh for the life of the world." This cements our faith in the Real Presence. Jesus is truly present in his flesh and blood, soul, and divinity in the Eucharist. What we see, what we touch, what we eat is the Lord. He gave his flesh for the life of the world and that flesh he gave is in the living bread that came from heaven.

Central to the reading is Jesus' assertion that their ancestors ate the manna in the desert but they died. When the manna was eaten, their ancestors were on a journey to the promised land. Jesus compares the manna to the bread of life to suggest that as the manna sustained their forefathers on their journey to the Promised Land, the living bread that came down from heaven is equally their sustenance on this life's journey. The difference is that whiles their ancestors ate the manna and died, whoever eats the living bread will have eternal life. The Eucharist then is our food for the journey. In these trying times, we should find our strength in the Eucharist. Bishop Walsh was imprisoned in China and was deprived of his access to his faith. According to him, a guard brought him a piece of a loaf and some wine daily. He wrote the words of consecration in between newspaper lines and putting the bread and wine in his palm, he celebrated Holy Mass as often as he could. He would also turn to the direction of HongKong daily, where he believed the Eucharist was celebrated and exposed and he knelt for long hours in adoration every day. He later attested that it was his celebration of the Eucharist and his long hours of distant daily adoration of the Blessed Sacrament that gave him the stamina to go through the rigors of his imprisonment.

In these difficult times when we are even deprived of our physical access to the Sacrament, the Eucharist continues to be our food for the journey. Wherever we are, we can turn to the direction where Jesus is exposed in all the tabernacles of the world and bend the knees in adoration and humble prayer. He will hear us, give us life and accord us the stamina to move on.

My Jesus, you are the bread that came down from heaven to accompany God's people in this earthly pilgrimage. In both easy and difficult times, may I find in you the sustenance that will give me the stamina to carry on and finally make it home to you.

FRIDAY OF THE THIRD WEEK OF EASTER

John 6:52-59

"...unless you eat the flesh of the Son of Man and
drink his blood, you have no life in you."

Friends, today we commemorate St. Joseph the Worker. My special interest
in this patron of mine would naturally make me do a reflection on him.
However, my wish to take up another reflection on the Eucharist is more
compelling. May I, therefore, ask St. Joseph to intercede for us all and
pray for justice and peace to prevail at our workplaces. May workers find
protection in the patron for workers and the jobless find a meaningful
job. May the jobs we do enhance our dignity as humans and enable us to
be instruments of charity and kindness to others. Happy feast day to all
Josephs and Josephines and Joes and Joeys. Bravo to all who join hands
with God in the business of renewing the face of the earth.

Leviticus 17:14 says, "You shall not eat the blood of any creature, for the
life of every creature is its blood." So why is Jesus asking that his body and
blood should be eaten? What is he insinuating? That his followers should
become cannibals? How was he going to give them his body and blood to
eat? Four times he says "eat my flesh, drink my blood." He does it a fifth
time and adds a promise: "just as the living Father sent me, and I have life
because of the father, whoever eats me will live because of me."

Jesus' choice of words doesn't depict him to be speaking in metaphors.
He is being real with his listeners. It is for this reason that the Jews are

puzzled: How can this man give us his flesh to eat? Theirs was a legitimate question. What they failed to see was that Jesus was not only man. He was true God and true man. Man though he was, he was also divine and since nothing is impossible for God to accomplish Jesus could indeed afford to ask the crowd to eat his flesh and drink his cup -(An institution he made at the Last Supper). He clarifies his flesh and blood statements by making a return to the bread from heaven discourse and contrasts the manna their forefathers ate in the desert with the living bread that gives life. In all this Jesus made clear the nature and the effects of the sacrament:

In its nature, the Eucharist is his flesh and his blood. The Eucharist is not a symbol of him but him. "Whoever eats me will have life because of me." Jesus is really and truly present in the Eucharist.

The effects of Eucharist are seen in the following:

a. I shall raise him on the last day

b. You will abide in me and I in you.

c. You will live because of me

d. You will live forever

Therefore, when we eat this bread and drink this cup we abide in him, he abides in us, he shall raise us up from death, we shall live because he lives and we shall have eternal life.

Friends in the Eucharist, Christ pledges his very life to us. In that pledge, he gives himself to us so we shall be united in him and have life forever. If we have no life in Jesus, then something must be lacking. St. Paul suggests that many of us are sick and some have have fallen asleep because of our approach to this all-important sacrament. He reminds us that if we eat the bread or drink the cup of the Lord in an unworthy manner we will be guilty of sinning against the body and blood of the Lord. He therefore, encourages us all to examine ourselves before we eat of the bread and drink from the cup. "For those who eat and drink without discerning the body of Christ eat and drink judgment on themselves (1 Corinthians 11:27-30).

May God forbid that the living bread he has sent from heaven to be the source and the summit of our life now and in eternity will become a means of judgment. Let us, therefore, respond positively to this generous offer of God with proper discernment and approach him not only with awe but also with humble and contrite hearts. For his life is ours for the taking.

Soul of Christ, sanctify me

Body of Christ, save me

Blood of Christ, inebriate me

Suffer me not to be separated from thee

From the malignant enemy defend me

In the hour of my death call me and bid me come to thee.

SATURDAY OF THE THIRD
WEEK OF EASTER

John 6:60-69

"Does this shake your faith?"

The sixth chapter of St. John's Gospel is packed with events and teaching. He fed the multitude with a poor lad's loaves and fish. He went up the mountain to be alone (most probably in prayer). He walked over the sea and calmed the raging storms. The signs he worked, especially for the sick, attracted the crowd to follow him from across the Sea of Galilee to Capernaum. At their arrival, Jesus challenges them to the real motive for their search of him. They had followed him just because they ate the bread and had their fill. He thereby exhorted them to work not for bread that perishes but for bread that leads to eternal life. From then on he began to teach them about the Bread of Life. In his teaching, Jesus made daring claims: I am the bread of life. I am the bread that came down from heaven. I came from God. No one has seen the Father except the one who came from the Father. I am the living bread. Whoever eats this bread will live forever. The bread I will give is my flesh for the life of the word. Whoever eats my flesh and drinks my blood will live. Whoever eats me will have eternal life. I will raise him up on the last day. No one can come to me except the Father draws him...

obviously, the people began to struggle with some of the claims Jesus made. How could he claim to have come from God when they knew his parents? How could he equate himself to God when he is a mere man? The law forbade the eating of a creature's blood, why would he suggest that his flesh and blood be eaten? Is he out flout the Law? And how could that be?

Though they were enthusiastic witnesses to the signs he worked and followed him on that account, Jesus' teaching shook the very foundation of the faith of all his listeners including his disciples. So they began to say, "This saying is hard; who can accept it?" Far from addressing their shock, Jesus compounds their situation by insinuating that they hadn't seen anything yet. One would think that knowing that they had difficulty believing what he taught, Jesus would make it easier for them to believe, but he did not. Rather be challenged them to wait till they saw his ascension, another difficult aspect of faith. At this point, he knows already who believed and who would betray him, and indeed those who did not believe left him and went back to their former way of life. It was at this point that Jesus turned to the Twelve and asked, "Do you also want to leave?" Simon Peter answered him, "Master, to whom shall we go? You have the words of eternal life. We have come to believe and are convinced that you are the Holy One of God."

Friends, today I am asking a number of questions:

a. What is it that shakes my faith?
b. Why didn't Jesus make it easier for his listeners to believe?
c. If I left my old self to embrace life in Jesus, what will I do if following Jesus gets tough? Will I abandon my faith?

There are happenings in life that shake our faith in God. There are encounters we make that threaten the roots of faith. Besides, there are many aspects of our faith that are hard to crack and digest. Even though faith seeks understanding, there are aspects of faith in God that reason cannot embrace. Sometimes we want to choose and pick what to believe and what not. However, faith is not always rational. Faith is also supra-rational. There comes a point in our faith life that reason is inadequate and so must give way to divine illumination. That is when we avail ourselves to the promptings of the Spirit and make a leap of faith. Remember Jesus made two important statements in the passage: it is the Spirit that gives life, the flesh is nothing. And no one comes to me except the Father draws him. So faith is a given. Faith is an act and a gift of God's Spirit. Faith comes to those who avail themselves. Those who in dark moments can put their hands into God's hands so God will hold them and lead the way. Otherwise when faith's foundations are shaken we backslide.

Faith also never comes easy. It is a mountain to scale. That is why Jesus never coaxed his listeners to faith. He is honest and sincere with them regarding matters of faith so that the enduring heart and mind will remain in faith even when its very foundations are shaken. So when we come to believe, it should be clear that we have not come to an easy ride. He has never promised that the journey of faith will be easy and he never will. However, he who is steadfast, will in spite of all odds, remain in him and hold on to his Word, for, he alone has the message of eternal life.

Is anything shaking our faith? Are we having a hard time with matters of faith? Are we tempted to make a return to a former unwholesome way of life because faith makes no sense any more? Let us never give up. This is the time to throw ourselves on God's Spirit and not depend on our human flesh. As his Spirit gives us life, the Father will draw us to the Son of Man, who alone has the message of eternal life.

My Jesus, in my faith crises, may nothing pluck me away from you, for it is only in you that I have redemption and you alone have the message of eternal life.

Fourth Sunday Of Easter

John 10:1-10

I am the gate

Friends, today is Good Shepherd Sunday. It is so because traditionally on this day we read from the 10th Chapter of John's Gospel. Owing to the day's character, it is known as vocations Sunday and we pray for all who have said yes to various vocations, especially for our pastors, priests, and religious.

As we do so, we reflect on aspects of the first ten verses of the chapter. St. John opens this chapter talking about the mode of entry into the sheepfold. One can either enter through the gate or not. The shepherd is the one who enters through the gate. He is a thief or a bandit if he enters through any other means. The shepherd enters when the gatekeeper opens the gate. He enters and calls his own by name and leads them out, going ahead of them. The sheep know his voice and come at his call. They never follow the stranger's voice. When the Pharisees failed to get his figure of speech, Jesus came out more clearly, saying, "I am the gate for the sheep." All the others were thieves and bandits and the sheep never listened to them. Jesus continued, "I am the gate. Whoever enters through me will be saved, and will come in and go out and find pasture. A thief comes only to steal and slaughter and destroy; I came so that they might have life and have it more abundantly."

Certain inferences could be made here and so much could be learned here. Let's note the following:

- shepherd enters through the gate. Thieves and bandits do not.
- The gatekeeper opens the gate for the shepherd
- I am the gate.

To this point, Jesus makes some deep revelations. The gate is the means through which the sheep distinguish shepherds from thieves and robbers. Jesus is the gate. Therefore, Jesus is the means to discerning who a true shepherd is. If my pastor is a true shepherd, I can only discern it in the light and illumination of Jesus. I believe that that same Jesus who makes a revelation of the true pastor to me is also capable of making a true shepherd for me. I should thus not only discern a true pastor, but I should also pray for Jesus to raise for me a shepherd after his own heart.

The shepherd can enter the sheepfold if the gatekeeper opens the gate. The gate is thus the only authoritative entrance the shepherd has. If the gate is not opened he has no access to his own sheep. Jesus is the gate. Jesus is that authoritative entrance of the shepherd, the only means through which the shepherd reaches out to the sheep in the fold.

As shepherds, we cannot make any meaningful access to the sheep, if we ignore the gate. Our pastoral successes reside in the gate who is Christ Jesus. Without him, therefore, the shepherd will only be that thief or robber who comes only to kill and destroy.

Next:

- He calls them each by name
- He leads them out and goes ahead of them

That the shepherd knows the sheep by name is also significant. To know one's name is to have a special relationship with the person. It is to have privileged access to the person's inner sentiments and thoughts. It is to have a special impact and certain control over the person. To know the name of the sheep is to have related well with the sheep, listened and learned from them, communicated as effectively with them as to have bought their confidence and to have had a positive influence on them.

The shepherd leads the sheep out, he goes ahead of them. He does not drive them, he rather leads them. He is a bad leader who drives and scatters the sheep where he is, the sheep scatter because they are unable to recognize his voice.

Finally:

- I am the gate
- Whoever enters through me will be saved
- He will come in and go out and will find pasture.
- I have come so they might have life in abundance.

Jesus is the I Am. I Am is God's name. Jesus the gate is God. Our salvation is in him. He gives life not only once and for all but always. Through him, the sheep are always nourished. Through the Gate, the sheep come in and go out to find pasture. Through the gate, the sheep are constantly maintained and sustained. He who brings nourishment brings life and he who brings abundant nourishment brings life to the full.

Jesus, therefore, is God. He determines the true shepherd and gives him access to the sheep. The shepherd knows the sheep by name and leads them constantly to greener pastures through Jesus who has come so we may have life to the full.

My Jesus, you are the Gate for the sheep. Help me to exercise my pastoral ministry through your promptings alone. And as I lead your sheep to pasture may they be nourished by you so they will attain the fullness of life.

MONDAY OF THE FOURTH WEEK OF EASTER

John 10:11-18

"I am the Good Shepherd."

In the early hours of John 10, Jesus says of himself, I am the gate for the sheep. Later on, he changed the metaphor, saying, I am the good shepherd. When he referred to himself as the gate, he contrasted between the shepherd and thieves and robbers. Here, the determining factor was the gate. When he changed the figure of speech, he contrasted between the Good Shepherd and the hireling. He distinguished them according to what they do and what they are. One knows the sheep and the sheep knows him. He lays down his life for the sheep. The other works for pay. He runs away at the scare of a wolf. So whiles one invests in the sheep, the other invests in himself. One is good both in what he does and what he is. The other could be good but to some extent, only in what he does for wages. To appreciate what Jesus is driving at, a look into the concept of the good could aid us.

Sharon M. Tan does a good job when she distinguished "good" as technical proficiency and "good" as a function of character. We can say a person is good to mean that the person is effective, efficient, or accurate in what he does. Such a person is apt in their profession and yield fitting results in whatever they do. Thus we can think of a good artisan or a good carpenter. Their goodness does not necessarily touch the person they are.

A good carpenter who makes exquisite furniture could, for instance, be a bad parent. What he is good at doing does not commensurate what he is.

Goodness can also be a function of character. Here, "good" is employed in reference to the person who lives a good life and has a consistent pattern of acting toward the common good. This goodness is always manifested in his relationships. In the context of Jesus' use of the "good", the good is not only the one who is proficient in technical skills but also consistently responds with an orientation toward the good. He is effectively good as well as good in virtue. This is the picture Jesus paints when he contrasts the Good Shepherd with the hired hand.

First of all, he says that the Good Shepherd lays down his life for the sheep. He also knows the sheep and the sheep knows him. The hired hand does not own the sheep. Because he works for pay, he runs for his life and leaves the sheep at the mercy of wolves.

What does it mean to lay down one's life? In this context, it could mean putting one's life in harm's way, taking a grave risk, exposing oneself to the danger of death, or even dying. To lay down one's life for the sheep then is to sacrifice oneself in the interest of the sheep. This can only be done by the one who has the skill to stand up to the wolf and fight for the sheep. To lay down one's life is also to forget oneself for the sake of another. It is to empty oneself of one's dignity and interests for the good of the other. This is an act of humility and humility is a function of character. According to John the Evangelist, love resides in his laying down his life for us (1 John 3:16). To lay down one's life then, is also an act of love. Jesus himself said that greater love no man has than to lay down his life for his friends. Laying down one's life is to act toward the good. It is both an act of proficiency and the practice of virtue. Jesus indeed is the Good shepherd. He is good by all standards. In saying I Am, he is God, and God is all in all Good.

Knowing the sheep and getting them to know you also come with a skill. The sheep will have nothing to do with you if you are not good at what you do with them. No sheep follows a fellow who merely pretends to feed it. For a sheep to follow, it must have built enough trust and a sense of security first. Knowing the sheep also implies having cut good relationships with them. It implies knowing their fears and aspirations, their joys, and sorrows. It is about knowing their needs and having the ability not only to address them but also to assure them that even the ordinary things he addresses in their lives are of utmost importance to him. Thus both in laying down his life and in knowing the sheep Jesus is the Good Shepherd. He is proficient in the skill of shepherding. He is also consistent in acting towards the good of the sheep. What he does for the sheep and what he is for the sheep coincide. He is simply The Good Shepherd.

Friends, as parents, teachers, politicians, priests, and professional workers, we are all shepherds. Even the individual who has no one to shepherd has himself or herself to shepherd. Jesus presents himself to us as the Good shepherd. The question is, are we anywhere close to the standard of leadership he sets for us? Do we invest in the sheep or we invest in ourselves? Are we mercenaries, working for wages or we attend to the sheep for love. Do I lay down my life for the sheep or I run away when my sheep are in danger of death-physically and spiritually. Do I know my sheep? Do they know me? Can I take after the Good Shepherd and allow a coincidence between what I am for my sheep and what I do for them?

My Jesus, you are the Good Shepherd and I want to be like you. May your goodness so abound in me that I may not only be found being good at what I do but also good in what I am for the sheep entrusted to my care.

Addendum To Fourth Week Of Easter

John 10:1-18

"The gatekeeper opens it for him."

According to John 10, the thief and the bandit do not enter the sheepfold through the gate. It is rather the shepherd who enters the sheepfold through the gate. He enters when the gatekeeper opens the gate for him. Jesus is the gate. Who then is the gatekeeper?

In Chapter 6 of John's Gospel, Jesus makes an assertion. According to him, no one can come to him except the Father who sent him draws him. For one to come to Jesus therefore, the one must have been drawn by the Father. In chapter 10, Jesus says, "I am the gate." When the Father draws one to Jesus, he draws the one to the gate. Jesus and the gate in this context are one and the same Person. This One Person is I AM. I AM is God. If a shepherd will enter the sheepfold, he must first come to the Gate and his coming to the Gate is engineered by the Father who draws him. The Father who draws the individual is I AM. He is God. If God the Father draws an individual to the Gate, and He intends the said individual to be a shepherd, that same power of God who draws the potential shepherd to the Gate could also be responsible for making it possible for him to enter not as a thief. Who then will the gatekeeper be?

In John 21:15-19, Jesus asked Peter three times if Peter loved him, and three times he also asked Peter to feed the flock. However, for Peter and the others to reach out to the sheep and feed them with the Word of God, it took the descent of the Holy Spirit on the day of Pentecost to accomplish that. We are told that they spoke as the Spirit gave them utterances and all heard them speak in their own native language. Like the sheep in John 10, they all recognized the voice of the shepherd and followed. That day many hearts were won and 3000 people got baptized. In Acts 11, Peter went to the Gentiles after a vision of assorted animals directed him there. For him to go to them, it was the Spirit that prompted him to go without discriminating. In his interactions there, it was only when the people received the baptism of the Spirit that Peter was emboldened to minister to them. Thus even though Peter had been asked by Jesus to shepherd the flock, it took the actions and the promptings of the Holy Spirit for him to enter into the hearts of the flock to feed them and to lead them to greener pastures. Who then will the gatekeeper be?

In my estimation, the Gatekeeper is the Father who draws us to the Son. The Gatekeeper is the Spirit who empowers, gives utterances to the shepherd, and makes the sheep receptive to the ministry of the shepherd. In the business of the Good Shepherd, therefore, I see one big divine event and a clear manifestation of the principle of perichoresis. The Father operates in the Son and the Spirit. The Son operates in the Father and the Spirit and the Spirit operates in the Father and the Son. There is a cordial divine dance in the Persons of the Trinity without any confusion or conflict. The ultimate aim there is for the sheep to have life and have it more abundantly. Jesus is the Gate, his Father draws us to him, the Spirit empowers whomsoever the Father draws and intends as a shepherd to enter the hearts of His faithful and by the power of His Word, Jesus Christ, lead them in and out to seek pasture.

TUESDAY OF THE FOURTH WEEK OF EASTER

John 10:22-30

"The works I do in my Father's name testify to me...
and no one can take them out of the Father's hand."

One of the songs I really enjoyed as a young seminarian was Loving Shepherd. A verse of that song said the following:

Loving shepherd of thy sheep

Keep me, Lord, in safety keeps

Nothing can thy power withstand

None can pluck me from thy side

This song echoes vividly something of the message of today's Gospel. The Jews are confused about Jesus and his message: I am the gate. I am the Good Shepherd. I lay down my life. I have come that they may have life and have it to the full etc. In their confused minds, they decide to ask Jesus to be forthright with them. Stop keeping us in suspense. If you are the Christ, tell us in plain words. Jesus tells them in reply, I have told you but you do not believe. However, the works I do in my father's name testify to me, yet, because you are not my sheep, you do not believe. He continued to say that my sheep recognize my voice. I know them, and they follow me. I give them eternal life. They shall never perish. No one can take them from my hands. Why? Because the Father gave them to me. The Father is greater than all. The Father has got them in his hands and no one can take them out of the Father's hands. He concluded saying, "The Father and I are one".

Friends today, I would like to underline two things:

a. The works that I do in my father's name testify to me.
b. No one can take them out of my hand

St. Pope Paul VI, once said that modern man listens more to witnesses than to teachers. If they listen to teachers, it because they are also witnesses. One day, a preacher was busily breaking his sweat pores to carry across his message. As he could hardly make any headway, someone in the audience whispered to a neighbor and said, "You know what! What he is and what he does speak so loudly to us that we all have difficulty hearing what he says." Today, Jesus drops a hint regarding the importance of backing one's discourse with works. All this while he has been teaching. Seven times, St. John records him as referring to himself as I AM. He did not only teach, but he also did a number of signs which could be done only by God or by the One sent from heaven. Therefore, when the Jews displayed gross lack of recognition of the meaning of what he said and the signs he worked and so demanded him to tell them in plain words if he is the Messiah, he nicely told them that telling them this once again will make no sense. This is because they are not His sheep and they will not recognize his voice if he told them who he really is. However, if they should look to the works he does in the Father's name they would know that he is the Messiah. In verse 38, Jesus would say that if I do these things and you do not believe me, at least believe in the works I do.

We carry our messages around every day. What we forget is that our audience hears us more from what we are and what we do in God's name than from what we say. Our mode of being, our manner of life, and the way we package and present ourselves are more compelling evidential pointers to the value of the message we bear than our word of mouth. As parents, priests, teachers, politicians, social leaders, and professionals, we make a better impact on others more by the witness of our lives than the words of mouth. If we will be believed, it is because we walk the talk we do in God's name.

Recognizing Jesus' voice and following him is a choice we make. When Peter and the three others heard Jesus' call at the seashore, nothing compelled them to leave their father and the boats to follow. They freely and willfully did so. Today, if we hear and recognize his voice and follow, it is because we have also freely chosen to. And He reassures us that if we make that choice, he will give us eternal life, we will not perish, we will put ourselves not only in his hands but also in his Father's hands. And nothing can pluck us out of the Father's hands.

Let us, therefore, walk the talk today and choose to recognize his voice and follow him like the sunflower follows the moments of the sun. He will keep us in safety keeps and nothing can take us out of his hands.

My Jesus, open my ears to your voice and my eyes to your works. May they grant me the grace to follow you in obedience, sincerity, and humility; so that I will forever enjoy the safety which your Father's hand alone can bring.

WEDNESDAY OF THE FOURTH WEEK OF EASTER

John 12:44-50

"Whoever believes in me believes not only in me but also in the one who sent me, and whoever sees me sees the one who sent me."

Today, we read from John 12:44 - 50. This forms part of Jesus' final discourse in John's gospel. Beyond it marks the beginning of his passion narrative. Like a teacher who concludes a course, Jesus sums up his mission on earth: He is the revelation of the father. Belief in him is tantamount to belief in the father. Seeing him is seeing the Father. He has come as light into the world so all who believe in him will never remain in the darkness. He has come to save the world and not to judge it. Rejecting him and his word brings about the judgment on the last day, to be executed by the very word he speaks. He speaks not of his own but as commanded by the Father. Since the Father's commandment is eternal life, Jesus speaks just as the Father has told him.

M. Moore-Keish, suggests that in this piece lies a brilliant outline of all the key teachings of Jesus in the eleven chapters before: light and darkness, judgment and eternal life, and the inextricable relationship between Jesus and the Father.

Of crucial significance to me is the sharp antithesis between Jesus' pointing to the Father as the source of his authority and at the same time pointing to his Coequality with the Father. At one moment he acknowledges that it is the Father that sent him and speaks according to the Father's commandment. At another moment, He identifies with the Father as one in being with him. If Jesus is one with the Father, then he does not necessarily need to point to the Father as the source of his authority. He has every reason to point to himself but he does not . Pointing to the Father is a sign of humility. Pointing to his identity with the Father is a sign of honesty. So Jesus tells the truth about himself. However, the important thing is that He tells the truth in humility. How beautiful would our world be if we could all learn to tell the truth to one another in humility and in kindness!

In this gospel, Christ also says three things:

a. I came into the world as light.
b. The word that I spoke will condemn him on the last day.
c. I speak the Father's commandment and his commandment is eternal life.

According to Jesus, He has come to save and not to judge the world. He has also come to speaks the Father's commandment of eternal life. Two things can bring us to eternal life: His light, which frees us from darkness, and His Word, when it does not condemn us. Thus in his Word and in his light, we shall have eternal life. If we ignore his light, we shall dwell in darkness and lose our way to eternal life. If we reject his word we will be judged by the word. We need Christ the light and Christ the Word to win eternal life. However, in Christ, the Light and the Word coincide. Light points the way and Word justifies us or condemns us. This is why it is important for all of us to light our paths to salvation with God's Word every day. He has inspired his word for our instruction regarding the truth and falsehood in our lives. His word corrects us when we go wrong and directs us to do what is right. His Word keeps us out of the darkness. Let us hold on to Jesus' Word and allow the illumination from the light of His Word to prevent our woeful condemnation on the last day.

Today, we resolve to tell the truth in humility and to renew our commitment to the Word of God as a light on our way to eternal life.

My Jesus, may the light of your Word lead me to the treasures of the truth. And when I have to speak the truth to a neighbor, grant me the spirit of humility to do so with kindness.

THURSDAY OF THE FOURTH WEEK OF EASTER

John 13:16-20

"The one who ate my bread has lifted his heel against me"

Today, we read from John 13:16-20. This is part of John's Last Supper setting. After he washed their feet, Jesus reminded the disciples that just as a slave cannot be greater than the master and a messenger not greater than the sender, they would be happy to understand what he had done and do the same. He reminded them also of his knowledge of those he had chosen. In doing so, he circled the betrayer and pointed him out as a fulfillment of scripture: The one who ate my food has raised his heel against me. He was saying this so when it happened they would that that he is I AM. He then assured them that their reception of him implied reception of him and of his Father.

I wish to delve into this statement of Jesus: The one who ate my bread has lifted his heel against me.

To raise one's heel against is to treat with contumely or contempt. It is to oppose or to become an enemy. It means treating another with insolence or unkindness.

But what has just happened? Jesus has just washed their feet. And someone among them has raised a heel against him. In my candid view, another way one could render the verse under consideration should be: One whose feet I just washed has raised his heel against me.

What did Jesus do when he washed their feet? He did a number of things:

He gave them an example of a Servant leader: he did what only a servant should do. Doing so, he presented himself as a leader who would stoop as low as a servant to be at their beck and call. He made himself all things to them.

He did a Self-emptying act: at a time when each of them felt too important to wash the feet of others, Jesus washed their feet. At the time when they were standing on their rights and dignity, Jesus shelved his own rights and dignity to wash their feet.

He made their feet beautiful. When he washed their feet, what Jesus did was to ready them to be bearers of the Word of God. As Scripture would have it, "How beautiful upon the mountain are the feet of those who bear the word of God!" By washing their feet, Jesus prepared them to be his ambassadors. This is why he could also say to them that whoever receives the one I send receives me and whoever receives me receives the one who sent me. In other words, he washed their feet so they would embody him as he goes back to the Father. He washed their feet so that they would indeed become God's household (see R. S. Baard).

Washing their feet, he showed them the debt of his love. By falling at their feet he poured abundant love on them. Scripture hast it that greater love no one has than to lay down his life for his friends.

The washing of their feet was thus a simple act that should have welled up nothing but great gratitude in the disciples. It should have taken a very hardened individual to use a foot so washed out of love to kick against such an agent of love. Painfully enough, a heel of the same feet Jesus washed was raised against him. A man who was shown such great love returned the love with betrayal. Perhaps, the washing of his feet should have turned things around for Judas. However, he was so engrossed in his evil intent that the light of love turned opaque to him.

Friends, very often, they are the ones who love us whom we hurt. The people we easily despise and treat with contempt are those who have washed our feet before. They sacrifice their rights and dignity, they empty themselves of their worth to make us only for us to unmake them. Some build us from grass to grace and all we do in return is to bring them to disgrace, pain, and hardship. God washes our feet every day. How do we respond to his feet-washing spree? Do we raise our heels against God?

In our day to day encounters, we wash feet and our feet are washed. What do we do with these mutual feet washings? In the Tempest, Shakespeare paints the character of a beast called Caliban. Caliban was tamed and taught to speak a language but he never ceased to be abusive. One day he said to his master, you taught me language and my profit on it is I know how to curse. In other words, you taught me language and I use it to insult you. When our feet have been washed, we do ourselves no service raising the heels of the same feet against them that washed us. Remember, Judas ended up taking his own life.

My Jesus, in this world of fragile peace and broken promises, may my heart never wander from the sense of appreciation I owe you and all who wash my feet every day. When I have been made, enable me to be thankful by lifting a finger to help build others.

Friday Of The Fourth Week Of Easter

John 14:1-6

"Do not let your hearts be troubled."

Friends, today, we read from John 14:1-6. This is a famous piece. We often hear it read at funerals. In it, Jesus at the Last Supper realizes how tensed his disciples were for fear of his imminent passion and death and their own impending betrayal and denial of him. He reassures them: Do not let your hearts be troubled. You trust in God, trust in me too. There are many mansions in my Fathers house. Had it not been so I wouldn't have told you. I will go and prepare a place for you and I will come back for you so that where I am you will also be. You know the way to where I'm going. Then Thomas objects. How can we know the way when we know not where? Jesus replies, I am the, the truth and the life. No one comes to the Father except through me.

Jesus makes certain emphatic statements here:

- Do not let your heart(s) be troubled.
- Trust in me
- There are many mansions in my Father's House
- I will go and prepare a place for you.
- I will come for you, you will be where I am.
- I am the way, the truth, and the life.

In the very first statement, there exists an exegetical detail that serves to throw light on what Jesus told his disciples. The English translation says,

Do not let your hearts be troubled." However, the Greek uses the word "Kardia" which translates as a heart. So what Jesus actually said was, Do not let your "heart" be troubled. Incidentally, the "your" Jesus uses before kardia is in the plural (see J. Clark-Soles). He was addressing all of them but making reference to one heart.

So what is Jesus saying? They who have accepted to be his disciples, though many, are one in heart. They may collectively or individually have their troubles, woes, tribulations, and snares but they should realize that they are in this together so their heart must not be troubled. It also means that none of them suffers alone. The anxiety of the individual is the anxiety of all. The distress of the group is the distress of everyone. In Christ Jesus, we are of one heart.

The question is: Can the church be said to be one in heart and mind and soul? Can our world be of one heart? Can the family be said to be of one heart? Can the husband and wife be said to be of one heart? Or each of us stands in isolation for himself or herself, expecting God to be for us all? Jesus was one with the Father and by promising us places in the many mansions in the Father's house, he underscores his union with the Father and his invitation to all of us to share in that substantial union he shares with the Father. However, that union begins with us here and now. One of the marks of the church is her oneness. Christ himself prayed that they may be one just as he and the Father are one. It is in that oneness that we are called. Christ unites us in heart and nothing should disintegrate that unity. In the salad bowl effect of discipleship, we may differ as individuals, yet we are made to be one in heart in Christ Jesus.

Many of the battles we wage would never be fought if we knew how much Christ desires us to be one in heart. Today, let us all resolve to be promoters and ambassadors of unity in Christ. If there is any step we can take to foster unity wherever we are, may we not be found wanting.

My Jesus, you came into the world to unite all things and all people in you. Whenever human ideologies and myopic thinking threaten to crack the unity in you, may your divine intervention cement our hearts together in you so that we shall share our joys and sorrows as one people with a common destiny in you.

SATURDAY OF THE FOURTH WEEK OF EASTER

John 14:7-14

Philip said to Jesus, "Master, show us the
Father, and that will be enough for us."

One of the deepest human desires is to see God. One of the songs we do in the Divine Office clearly expresses this sentiment when it says: It were my soul's desire to see the face of God. It were my soul's desire to rest in his abode." In trying times, in times of hardships and disappointments, when we lose a loved one, in sickness and in economic crises, the human cry has often been: "where is our God?" One philosophy professor of mine once asked, "where was God in the times of Auschwitz?" I believe in our own privacy we have had to battle with the quest to see God's face in certain circumstances of life.

In our gospel reading today, Philip renews that quest for God. He does so to satisfy not only his individual curiosity but for the satisfaction of all. Lord, show us the Father and we shall be satisfied. Philip makes a number of appearances in John's gospel, at least four times. Two out of these times, the word satisfaction is on his lips. One time he thinks about the satisfaction of others (two hundred days wages will not be enough to buy bread to satisfy this crowd), another time, he thinks of the satisfaction of all. He seeks that which satisfies the many. He suggests that true satisfaction rests in the manifestation of the Father. Jesus, a little surprised at his lack of insight and vision after being with him all this while, affirmed: "he who has seen me has seen the Father." Jesus is the self-revelation of the Father. The Father reveals himself to us through Jesus. Jesus should, therefore, be our satisfaction. The Father is in him and he is in the Father. We know him by sight, by his words, and by his works. He calls us to believe in him in order to have life, and that even if we would not believe him on account of his presence and his words, we should believe him because of his works. For Jesus therefore, his works are a sure sign of his revelation of the Father.

What are some of his works?

- He changed water into wine
- He healed the Royal Official's Son
- He healed the paralytic at the pool of Bethesda
- He fed the five thousand
- He walked on the sea
- He restored sight to the man born blind.
- He raised Lazarus from death.

These works of Jesus point to him and ultimately reveal the Father. He who believes in him would be accomplishing these works and even more because as Jesus goes to the Father, he continues to glorify the Father in himself by hearing our every supplication and enabling us to do the works he does and even greater.

Jesus reveals the Father. He reveals the Father conspicuously in the works he does. Those who believe because of his works would do the same works and more because Jesus would do whatever we ask. Since the works which does serve as a sure manifestation of him and the glorification of the Father in him would be enabled in his believers, Christ and for that matter, his Father will always be revealed in the works which his believers will accomplish by the help of him who hears our prayers.

Where then is our God? God is in Jesus as Jesus is in Him. He is manifested to us in our sight of Jesus, and in Jesus' words but above all in his works. Because his works and even greater will be accomplished by those who believe, God is still revealed in the works he enables in his faithful ones. Thus whenever joy and abundance replace embarrassment and scarcity,

God is made manifest. When there is unexpected healing, and paralysis gives way to movement, our God is revealed. When the hungry are fed and filled; when the raging storms of life are stilled, God's hand is at work. When new vision and insight are given and life triumphs over death, it is the same Jesus who reveals the Father by hearing our prayer and enabling his works in us because we believe (see Craig. A. Satterlee).

Our God is made manifest in His Son. The Son is revealed in His real presence, in his words, and in his works. His works are sure signs of his union with the Father. The same works and more, he enables in all who believe in him. In the perpetuation of God's works among us, God continues to be revealed to us. By the power of his hand at work in our midst, our God is never hidden. He is as close to us today as Jesus was to his disciples two thousand years ago.

My Jesus, you are ready to do for me all that I ask the Father in your name. Reinforce my belief in you and enable your good works in me so that through my little kindness, your father's love may be experienced and realized in my neighbor.

MONDAY OF THE FIFTH WEEK OF EASTER

> "Whoever has my commandments and
> observes them is the one who loves me."

What does it mean to love? If someone should ask, Do you love God or do you love me? What will the person be looking for?

In the theology of St. John the Evangelist, love is in obedience to the commandments (1 John 5:3). Jesus reiterates this definition when he says, Whoever has my commandments and observes them is the one who loves me. Obedience to Jesus' commandments is, therefore, loving Jesus. What is Jesus' Commandment? Earlier in John's Gospel Jesus said,

"I give you a new commandment, that you love one another. Just as I have loved you, you also should love one another. By this everyone will know that you are my disciples if you have love for one another" (13:34–35). Later on, he would also say,

"This is my commandment, that you love one another as I have loved you. No one has greater love than this, to lay down one's life for one's friends" (15:12–13).

Logically speaking, to love is to obey Jesus' commandment, and to obey the commandment is to love Jesus. Restating Jesus' words above, we can say, "If one loves me, then he has my commandments and observes them." Putting Jesus' words in a conditional statement gives it a new character. In a conditional statement, there is a necessary condition and sufficient condition (see C. A. Satterlee). For Jesus then, it is necessary to have his commandments and observe them in order to do that which is sufficient, ie, to love. Loving Jesus here is a sufficient condition. If the commandments and their observance (necessary condition) constitute love and love of Jesus is the sufficient condition for being a disciple, then in the true disciple of Jesus, the necessary condition and the sufficient condition must coincide.

In the metaphysics of being, the coincidence of the necessary and sufficient conditions in an individual being defines the mode of existence of that individual being. Therefore, my way of being resides in the coincidence of that which is sufficient and that which is necessary for me to be what I am.

What Jesus is saying here is that his true disciple is the one in whom is found simultaneously His commandments and obedience to them (which is love) on the one hand and the love of him on the other. To obey the commandments is to love him and to love him is to obey his commandments. Love must, therefore, exist in its full blossoming in a true disciple of Jesus, simply because he does not only love Jesus but also keeps his commandments. Jesus continues to indicate that, in the fullness of love is the Father's affection and in the fullness of love is Jesus' own affection and self-revelation. As he puts it, "Whoever loves me will be loved by my Father, and I will love him and reveal myself to him." He later affirms that with the same fullness of love is not only the affection of the Father and the Son but also the indwelling of the divine Godhead: "Whoever loves me will keep my word, and my Father will love him, and we will come to him and make our dwelling with him." When love dwells in us in all its richness, when we possess and observe the commandments of God, He makes His own love abound in us as He makes a dwelling in us.

Today, I wish to encourage us to reflect on our way of being: How am I defined in my mode of being?

- Do I reflect love in all its fullness?
- How much of Jesus' Commandments do I have in me?
- How much of it do I observe?
- Does the Father love me?
- Does the Son love me?

- Does the Son reveal himself to me?
- Will God freely come to me and make a dwelling in me?

Whoever loves me will keep my word. My Father will him, I will love him. We shall come to him and make a dwelling with him.

May the Holy Spirit be our guide today, may He teach us to love and give us the strength to embrace the commandments of love and live in obedience to them. May we all be fashioned in our beings to be instruments of love.

TUESDAY OF THE FIFTH WEEK OF EASTER

John 14:27-31a

> "...the ruler of the world is coming.
> He has no power over me..."

We continue to read from Jesus' farewell discourse. We reflect today on John 14:27-31a.

After encouraging love and obedience to the law in his disciples, Jesus gave them the gift of peace. In his own words, "Peace I leave with you; my peace I give to you. Not as the world gives do I give it to you." He then exhorted them not to be afraid or let their hearts be troubled. Why would their hearts be troubled? Because very soon Jesus would go away. He describes his going away as going to the Father, which should make them happy. If he is going to the Father, why would the disciples be troubled? They would be troubled because Jesus could not go to the Father without going the way of the Cross. This is why he also said, "...the ruler of the world is coming." The way of the Cross is such a venomous path to take that Jesus' Passion and death would seem like evil has conquered the Good. However, the truth is that evil has no power over Jesus. Evil might reign momentarily but what conquers all is the love of the Father. The Cross is, therefore, Jesus' expression of love and obedience to the Father's command. In the Cross, the ruler of the world will be conquered and Jesus will return to his glory. This is why their hearts should not be troubled. This is why his lasting peace must reign in their hearts.

Friends, today, Jesus makes a number of allusions:

- I leave you peace, my own peace I give you
- Do not let your hearts be troubled or afraid
- I am going away and I will be back
- Rejoice that I go to the father if you love me
- The Father is greater than I
- The ruler of this world has no power over me
- I love the Father and do what He commands me.

It is heartwarming to see that Jesus, the one who is going to die wishes peace not unto himself but to his friends who would be troubled by the seeming triumph of evil. Here, Jesus puts his own distress aside and extends shalom, divine blessings that result in the completeness of others. Jesus' peace offering here is an act of self-forgetfulness, an act of selflessness and magnanimity. How often have I not looked for my own peace when I could have gone the extra mile to bring peace and tranquility to others! Fear destroys, fear incapacitates, fear tears apart. When Jesus wished the disciples peace before his own passion, he allayed their fears, he anticipated their inner destruction and made them whole. He showed a keen interest in their total wellbeing.

Jesus also intimates that the ruler of this world is real. He operates and can prevail but he has no power over Him. He is the Son of the Father who is greater than all and evil cannot be greater than God. Whenever evil, as vicious as the way of the Cross, seems to hold sway in our lives, our hearts need not be troubled. We serve a God over whom evil has no power. If we love him and obey his commands He is faithful to deliver us for the glory of his name. Sometimes, the evil we suffer should make us glad because, like Jesus, the Cross is the road to the Father.

Finally, Jesus presents himself to be practicing what he teaches. Hitherto, he told his disciples that anyone who has my commandments and observes them loves me. In this piece, he says, "the ruler of the world is coming. He has no power over me, but the world must know that I love the Father and that I do just as the Father has commanded me." The world must thus know that Jesus is the epitome of what he demands of his disciples. He does not teach one thing and do something else. He loves the Father and does what the Father commands him to do. His true disciple is the one who loves him and keeps his commandments. As priests, parents, teachers, socio-political leaders, how often have we demanded something of others but have acted to the contrary? What great impact shall we make if we were to practice what we preach! Jesus has opened the way for us today.

We underline the following for our reflection:

Jesus is pleased to put our interests over and above his own.

The ruler of the world has no power over him.

Evil has only a momentary power but the love of God conquers all.

Jesus makes no demands he doesn't mean to keep.

My Jesus, you hold the whole world in your hands and the ruler of the world has no power over you. When I am assailed by the power of darkness, may your love for me transform every evil I face into good for the glory of your name.

WEDNESDAY OF THE FIFTH WEEK OF EASTER

John 15:1-8

"I am the true vine, and my Father is the vine grower. He takes away every branch in me that does not bear fruit, and everyone that does he prunes so that it bears more fruit."

Today, St. John the Evangelist reminds us of Jesus as the true vine, we as the branches and his Father as the vinedresser. The branch has the vocation to bear fruit. It achieves this goal chiefly by maintaining an unbroken contact with the vine and also by succumbing to the pruning of the vinedresser. Its success as a branch thus depends not only on its attachment to the vine but also on the effective pruning of the gardener.

Perhaps you know the story of the busy businessman who desired to plant a garden. He hired an experienced horticulturist who was also well versed in landscaping to begin the garden. Owing to his busy schedule and his inability to keep up the garden, he made a request for a maintenance-free garden with automatic sprinklers and other labor-saving devices. To his utter disappointment, the horticulturist told him, "There's one thing you need to know and deal with before we go any further. If there's no gardener, there's no garden!"

Many are the branches who desire to bear fruit but hardly would want the painful process of pruning. They therefore would want to suck the sap of the vine and grow but would want to have nothing to do with the vine dresser. For many such people, God, the vinedresser, is so intolerable to man that man should want to have nothing to do with him. However, by referring to the Father as the gardener, Jesus underscores the importance of God in the fruit bearing business of the branch. He points to the various ways God can prune our lives to make us even more fruitful than we presently are.

Admittedly, there are certain things we may need to shed if we are to become all that God has called us to be. We need some kind of letting go, which though currently painful, can help us to grow eventually in our relationship with God and with others. Through all the experiences of pruning in our lives, the Lord never leaves us. He is near to us. He makes his home in us, he remains in us. We therefore, don't have to endure being pruned on our own. The same Lord who makes his home in us sustains us in those times, and leads us into a new and a more fruitful life. However, for this to happen, we need to remain in him as he remains in us. Let us therefore renew our commitment to Prayer, the sacraments, loving obedience, and suffering in union with Christ. In this commitment, we shall remain united to the vine; in this, we shall keep the Christian sap flowing in our lives; and as we grow in faith, the Father's mastery pruning will make us as fruitful as we have been called to be.

My Jesus, you are the Vine and I am your branch. Let nothing separate me from you. May I remain so firmly in you that I will avail myself to the Father's pruning which alone can make me what I am meant to be.

THURSDAY OF THE FIFTH WEEK OF EASTER

John 15: 9-11

"This is my commandment: love one another as I love you."

Not quite long ago, I read a simple story that made a lasting impression on me. It tells of a group of businessmen who attended a workshop in a faraway city. They had assured their families that they would be home early enough for Saturday night's dinner. As they rushed through the airport at the end of the workshop, one of them inadvertently kicked over a table that held a display of oranges and mangoes. Oranges and mangoes flew and scattered everywhere. Without stopping or looking back, they all managed to reach the plane, just in time. All but one- Bill. Bill told the others to go on without him. He returned to where the oranges and mangoes were all over the floor. He was indeed glad he did. The 15-year-old girl, the orange seller, was totally blind! She was softly crying, tears running down her cheeks. As she groped for her spilled produce, the crowd swirled about her and everyone rushed to their flights.

Bill knelt on the floor with her, gathered up the fruits, put them back on the table, and helped reorganize her display. He set aside the bruised and battered mangoes in a separate basket. When he had finished, he pulled out his wallet and said to the girl, "Here, please take this $50 for the damage we did. Are you okay?" She nodded through her tears. He continued, "I hope we didn't spoil your day too badly."

As Bill started to walk away, the bewildered blind girl called out to him,

"Sir...."

He paused and turned to look back.

She continued, "Are you, Jesus?"

Bill couldn't get that question out of his head for days. It was such a simple, small-scale event, but it made him see clearly what following Christ was really all about.

To follow Jesus is to love. He himself calls on us in today's gospel to "Love one another as I have loved you." Love is the identity of a Christian. To be a Christian is to be another Christ. To be another Christ is to love.

The Greek language has various words for love. Storge refers to familial love. It is the love between parents and children. Eros is the love of attraction between man and woman. Philia is the love of friendship. These describe the love that points to humanity. They are basically horizontal in their dimensions. However, there is love that is both horizontal and vertical. It is so because much as it has an interest in human good, it also points to the divine. Such is Agape love.

Agape is love as goodwill, benevolent love that cannot be conquered, a love that wills only the good for the person loved. In his book, Love and Responsibility, Karol Wojtyla (Pope John Paul II), remarks that to love someone with truly benevolent love is to will God for them since God is the supreme good of each human person. St. Augustine throws better light on the discourse on love when he said that this love is distinguished from men's love for each other as men. According to him, Christ made this distinction by not merely asking us to love one another, but by adding, "As I have loved you." Christ loves us to the extent that we should reign with Him. He calls us to so love one another that our love will be different from that of other men, who only love one another for the sake of it. We can give only what we have. I cannot will to another what I do not have. If loving someone means willing God to them, then my love for them implies that I myself have God, that I love God and my extension of love towards them is to the end that God may be discovered and loved in them. Loving as Christ has loved us is thus loving for the sake of God. St. Augustine would, therefore, say, "They who love one another for the sake of having God within them, they truly love one another." My love for you should make you experience God's awesome presence and cultivate in you, love for God and neighbor. It is precisely love as agape that Christ asks from every one of us when He commands us to love one another.

Today, we would like to meditate on whether people we encounter in our daily lives really find genuine love which points to Christ and generates in them a true love for God and neighbor.

My Jesus, you are love and your command to me is to love as you do. May the help of your grace instill in me love that knows no ending, that in my daily encounters I will reflect nothing but the love that would cut the path for others to the knowledge of you and the love of neighbor.

FRIDAY OF THE FIFTH WEEK OF EASTER

John 15:12-17

"This I command you: love one another."

Today, I salute all our Farmers as we celebrate St. Isidore the Farmer. Through his intercession, may our farmers be granted good health and all the favorable conditions needed for a successful season. May their hard work be duly rewarded, their dignity enhanced and the fruit of their labor bring hope and consolation to the poor and needy in society.

We continue reading John 15. Verses 12-17 which constitute our subject for reflection make love and friendship the focus. Jesus commands us to love. He defines greater love to be found in laying down one's life for one's friends. He redefines his relationship with his disciples as he elevates them from the status of slaves to friends. His reason for this new definition is tangent to his making known to them all he has heard from the Father and having revealed to them all he does. He turns the tables of friendship procedure upside down as he underscores himself as the agent of choice in his friendship with them. "It was not you who chose me, but I who chose you". He also appointed them to bear fruit that will last. In their fruitfulness, the Father will give them all they ask for in Jesus' name.

As I read this text, certain questions kept running through my mind:

a. Can love be commanded?
b. Why would Jesus command us to love?
c. Why is Jesus insisting on his choosing his friends?

Many of us grew up in a culture that looked on love as a sentiment, an emotion, or an effusive expression of some cosmetic charity. Such sentimentality can only be aroused or gingered in me. As it is love that spontaneously springs from the heart it can hardly be commanded. As a matter of fact, any attempt at commanding such sentimental love or forcing it out of another only ends up in indifference. Indifference breaks down relationships and what is supposed to be love hardly bears any fruits.

So what was Jesus doing when he said, "This I command you: love one another."? Jesus commands love that is patterned on the love between him and his Father. God's love is what Jesus commands. It is love that transcends emotions and sentiments. It is because God's love is love in action and not in feeling that Jesus commands it. According to E. Askew, "The definition of God's love is God's actions." She believes that the definitions of God's love that we have access to are its results: God's love creates, God's love redeems, God's love bears fruit, God's love lays down its life. For her, "God's love is that which creates something new, restores what has been broken, completes what is unfinished, heals what has been hurt, and gives itself to the point of death." Such is the love that Jesus commands.

In obedience to Jesus' command, therefore, to say " I love you" to someone else is to certify that I will do something positively new in their lives; that I will act so as to restore their brokenness and fill the emptiness in their lives; that I will nurse their wounds and heal their pains; that I will sacrifice my life just so that the other will live. It takes nothing but the Father's hand to accomplish these. This is why Jesus would remind them that if they bore fruit in love, the Father will grant all they ask for in his name.

Jesus also insists, "It was not you who chose me, but I who chose you ." He is calling them friends, why must he insist on how their friendship was established? Jesus says nothing for nothing. He neither does nothing for nothing. If he insists, he does so for a reason. In the Greco-Roman context, it was customary that pupils chose their master, not vice versa (see Luis Menendez-Antuña). So if Jesus loved them, chose them, and elevated them from slaves to friends, he must have done so to drive home a lesson. Jesus seems to be saying here that it is not important for everyone to love us. It is much more important that we love everyone as he has loved us.

Many a time, we look for love and friendship rather than giving one. Whenever we insisted on being loved, we locked ourselves up in a cage only to collude with like-minded people who think and behave like us but lack the courage to build us up and point us to God. Jesus gave love, he offered friendship. He did so to remind us that true love and true friendship reside not in like-mindedness but in Christ-mindedness. The Christ-minded gives love and offers friendship. Jesus therefore, gives us an example of giving love which is an act of total self transformation and a means to sourcing the Father's providence. When God so loved the world, he gave. When Jesus loved the disciples, he chose them. Love in us should make us act as well.

My Jesus, in obedience to your command, may I give love and offer friendship to others the way you would. Make me an instrument of your actions in their lives so that together we may bear fruits that will last.

SATURDAY OF THE FIFTH WEEK OF EASTER

John 15:18-21

"...you do not belong to the world, and I
have chosen you out of the world..."

Consider the statement: It is insane to be sane when the whole world is insane. This statement, as we can see, assumes that all of us are called to stand in solidarity with the world. We should therefore rise and fall with the world. Worldly standards should so be the yardstick for our morality and lives of virtue that should the world be insane, our own sanity will be deemed insanity because we would be standing in contradistinction to the values of the world.

The question is: Do we belong to the world? Must we be ruled by worldly values and standards?

Jesus answers this question in John 15:19. According to him, we do not belong to the world. He has chosen us out of the world. That being the case, we are ruled by values and standards different and higher than those of the world. We are, therefore, called not conform our lives to worldly values. For Jesus then, it is sane to be sane when the whole world is insane. Being sane in the midst of the world's insanity would definitely attract the world's displeasure. This is because the world loves its own. The world promotes those who flow with its tide. The world champions they who dance to its tunes. The world would, therefore, hate us if we live by Jesus' standards. Nevertheless, the hatred of the world should be evidence of the goodness of the true friend of Christ. This is the bell Jesus rings when he says that if the world hates you, realize that it hated me first. If you belonged to the world, the world would love its own; but because you do not belong to the world, and I have chosen you out of the world, the world hates you. Jesus calls us to set our standards and values over and above all worldly standards. He seems to be asking us to set our hearts on his own values and please God rather than stand in solidarity with the world. St. Gregory would say that there is nothing wrong with not pleasing those who do not please God. We are not God's friends if we please God's enemy. The truth is that when we subject our souls to the Truth, we will have to contend with the enemies of that Truth (see St. Gregory). This is why Jesus, knowing that his true friends would be hated by the world, consoled them, saying that if the world hates you, realize that it hated me first and that no slave is greater than his master. If they persecuted me, they will also persecute you.

We are in the world, but we are not of the world. As Christians, Jesus is our model for values and morals. He is the Way, the Truth, and the Life. When he lived the Truth he contradicted all worldly unwholesome values and the world hated and persecuted him. In his passion, he laid the pathway for us to follow. He is the same Jesus who has chosen us to live in solidarity with him and not with the world. When the world champions negative values, we are true friends of God when we seek what is above. Doing so, we might incur the world's displeasure but we would never be the first, neither shall we be the last to suffer. He himself suffered it for the glory of the Father and so it is better for us who follow him to please God than to please men.

Let everyone today think of a single value that the world cherishes.

In the face of that worldly value, what choice would you make?

Would the world love or hate you for the choice you will make?

Will that choice make you a friend or an enemy of God?

Lord Jesus, you were hated and persecuted for the Truth, may I not fail to submit my soul to that Truth even if it brings me pain and hatred from the world. May I nail my own passion on account of your truth to your Cross so that on the last day, I will live with you in your glory.

MONDAY OF THE SIXTH WEEK OF EASTER

John 15:26b -16:4a

"When the Advocate comes whom I will send you
from the Father, the Spirit of truth who proceeds
from the Father, he will testify to me."

Today we read from John 15:26b-16:4a. This excerpt forms a crucial part
of all we believe as Christians.

In the Nicene Creed, the Church professes faith in the Holy Spirit, the
Lord, the Giver of life, who proceeds from the Father and the Son.

The importance of the Holy Spirit in the life of every Christian can not
be overemphasized. In his farewell discourse, Jesus variously mentions
and promises of the Spirit to his disciples. Up until John 15: 26b he had
made such statements three times. In John 14:16-17, Jesus made the first
announcement of the coming of the Paraclete. He introduced the Spirit
as the one whom the Father sends to abide in the hearts of the disciples.
In 14:26, the Father will send the Paraclete to teach them everything and
remind them of all that Jesus had said to them. The Spirit would thus
assist and enable them to address their present circumstances. In chapter
15:26-27, Jesus reiterates the discourse on the Paraclete. This time around,
he himself will send the Advocate from the Father. He is the Spirit of truth
who proceeds from the Father. He will testify to Jesus. Jesus then makes a
curious statement, "And you also testify, because you have been with me

from the beginning." Is there a link between the testimony of the Spirit to Jesus and that of the disciples? I wonder.

Well, Jesus goes on to tell them his reasons for telling them about the Advocate.

a. So that they would not fall away.
b. Because they would be expelled from the synagogues.
c. On the pretext of worshiping God, people will put them to death.
d. Out of ignorance of the Father and the Son, the disciples would be mistreated.

Friends, today's passage schools us on the Holy Spirit and his relationship with the Father and the Son.

- Who is the Holy Spirit?
- Why will the Spirit testify to Jesus and the disciples must testify too because they had been with Jesus?
- Will being with Jesus be synonymous with being with the Spiritual?
- What link is there between the Spirit, Jesus, and the Father?

Simply put, The Holy Spirit is the third Person in the Godhead. According to our reading, he is the Paraclete. Literally speaking a parakletos is one called to the side of another as an advocate. He is a counselor, a witness, one who speaks on another's behalf and testifies on account of him/her. He coaches one as to how to stand up in one's own defense. He gives the wisdom and the courage to his clients to be confident before the judgment seat. He is the comforter.

Before parting with his friends, Jesus knew that they would suffer persecutions and martyrdom. He knew they would go into faith crisis. He, therefore, promised them the Paraclete so that in those trying moments they would remain steadfast in their faith. He was unequivocal on that: "I have told you this so that you may not fall away." The Holy Spirit is thus the one who keeps us in faith and in shape when troubles come and our hearts are burdened. He enables us to be true witnesses to Jesus in season and out of season.

But the Holy Spirit is not isolated from God. He is not less than God. He is God. Remember what Jesus said, "...the Advocate whom I will send from the Father. The Spirit of truth who proceeds from the Father."

Jesus is the One sending the Advocate.

Jesus is sending the Advocate from the Father.

The Advocate is the Spirit of truth.

Jesus is the Way, the Truth, and the Life.

The Spirit of Truth is, therefore, the Spirit of Jesus.

The Spirit of Truth proceeds from the Father.

Therefore, the Spirit is of the Father and of the Son.

What Jesus promised the disciples, therefore, is God's own abiding presence in the Person of the Holy Spirit who is our Paraclete.

What he promised the disciples of old, he promises us too. We need the Holy Spirit today more than ever before. We need him to rush upon us and abide in us. We need him to stand by us and plead our cause. We need him to instruct our hearts and grant us his sevenfold gifts of Wisdom and knowledge, understanding and counsel, wonder and recognition, and awe (see The Spirit Psalm). We need the Spirit at all times and in all climes.

Come Holy Spirit. Fill the hearts of your faithful and kindle in us the fire of your love. Send forth your Spirit and we shall be created and you shall renew the face of the earth.

TUESDAY OF THE SIXTH WEEK OF EASTER

John 16:5-11

"And when he comes he will convict the world in regard
to sin and righteousness and condemnation."

We read today from John 16:5-11.

The disciples of Jesus had many reasons to be downcast at the thought of Jesus' parting. Today, the impact of his departure on them is so palpable and their grief so real that Jesus takes the trouble to school them of the benefits of his going to the Father. He tells them the following truth: "it is better for you that I go. For if I do not go, the Advocate will not come to you. But if I go, I will send him to you." Jesus then enumerates some of the things the Spirit would accomplish: He will convict the world with regard to sin, righteousness, and judgment.

- Sin because the world does not believe in Jesus
- Righteousness because Jesus is going to the Father
- Condemnation because the ruler of the world has been conquered.

William Barclay gives an insight into understanding this passage. He places the key to comprehending the text in the Greek word Elegchein. This word which Jesus employs here translates in English either as convict or convince. It is generally used in prosecutorial situations. Imagine a court situation where the prosecutor asks loaded questions to elicit the truth from a suspect. The suspect is slowly brought to the realization that something he did was not right. That realization brings the suspect to the conviction that what he did was wrong. In this case, what the prosecutor has done is to convince the suspect regarding the error he has made. The error that is convinced in the suspect could also convict him. Realizing an error might lead to the admission of guilt which might convict the suspect. In this case, the prosecutor would not only have convinced the suspect but would have also convicted him. For Jesus then the Holy Spirit will come after him to prosecute the world and this would be to the advantage of his disciples. He would convict and convince the world for sin, on righteousness and condemnation.

In the beginning of his Gospel, St. John says that Jesus came to his own but his own did not receive him, but those who received him were given the power to become children of God. Sin is that which makes us depart from God. Through Jesus, we are made children of God. When we fail to believe in Jesus and accept him, we draw a wedge between ourselves and God. We fall into sin. It takes the Holy Spirit to convict us of this sin. This is what happened in the life and passion of Jesus. When the people failed to accept him; when they chose Barabas over Jesus; when they put him to death on the Cross, all they did was to separate themselves from God. When the day of Pentecost had come and the disciples had received the outpouring of the Spirit, in the power of the same Spirit, they convicted the world of the sin of unbelief and convinced their audience that they acted out of ignorance when they put the Righteous One to death (see Acts of the Apostles). As the Spirit, acting through the Apostles convicted them of their sins and convinced them of Jesus' Righteousness, many became believers, asking, what must we do in order to be saved (see Acts 2:37-41). They turned from their former ways into newness of life. So what Jesus is saying here is that the Spirit coming after him will bring transformation into the world.

The Spirit also captivates and convinces the world on Jesus' righteousness. This according to Jesus is because he (Jesus) goes to the Father. How was Jesus to go to the Father? If the Cross is the way to the Father, then Jesus was going to the Father by the Way of the Cross. We remember that it was while Jesus was on the Cross that the Centurion declared that indeed this man was the Son of God. This Centurion represents a world that is captivated. The power of the Passion and the grace of the dying Jesus took hold of him such that what he uttered could only have come from the power of the Spirit. As a matter of fact, it only takes someone imbued by the Spirit to be so convicted by the Christ-event to convincingly acclaimed a condemned individual as the Son of God. If Jesus was the Son of God, then the world was wrong in condemning the Righteous one to a shameful death. The world can come to this admission only through the power of the Spirit.

The Spirit also convinces the world because the ruler of the world has been condemned. The last time Jesus made reference to the ruler of the world, he said that the ruler of the world had no power over him. He said that to suggest that even if evil thrives, it will never have the last word. His three days in the tomb and his resurrection are pointers to the fact that death had been defeated and victory had been won. It took the outpouring of the Holy Spirit and the ministry of the apostles for the world to be convicted and convinced that evil had no longer power over the world and that all who die and are raised with him are a new creation.

The Spirit convicts and convinces. He transforms our world and reveals to us the righteousness of God. He convinces us that in Christ, evil has no power over the world. May we be affected by Spirit's promptings so that captivated by the paschal mystery and convinced of the Power of Jesus, we might escape the attractions of the evil one, and live lives of righteousness, devoid of sin.

Come Holy Spirit. Cleanse me from sin. Reveal to me the righteousness of God and enable me to cling to him who alone has the power to rule the World.

WEDNESDAY OF THE SIXTH WEEK OF EASTER

John 16:12-15

"But when he comes, the Spirit of truth,
he will guide you to all truth."

The excerpt for our reflection today is from John 16:12-15. This piece continues Jesus' exposé on the Holy Spirit. Till now he has revealed the Spirit as the Paraclete, the one called to stand by us as our Advocate. He has also revealed him as the prosecutor of the world who convinces and yet convicts the world of sin, righteousness, and condemnation. Today, he makes further revelations on the Spirit:

- He is the Spirit of truth.
- He will guide you to all truth.
- He will not speak on his own, but he will speak what he hears.
- He will declare to you the things that are coming.
- He will glorify me because he will take from what is mine and declare it to you.
- Everything that the Father has is mine.

Friends, it is fascinating how Jesus spares no effort to make clear to his disciples the fact of the unity of the Father, the Son, and the Spirit. If Jesus is the Truth then the Spirit of truth is the Spirit of Jesus. The Spirit will speak what he hears, he will also take what belongs to Jesus and declare to the disciples. What the Spirit takes and declares from Jesus is from the

Father. For "Everything that the Father has is mine." The Spirit is mine, he takes and gives what is mine, what is mine is my Father's because everything the Father has is mine.

Having underscored the oneness of the Trinity, Jesus also reveals to them what the Spirit of truth will accomplish in them: He will guide them to all truth. Jesus does a brilliant play on words here. The Greek he uses is hodēgeō, which literally translates as "to lead on the way." (See T. D. Stegman). Literally speaking, Jesus said that when the Spirit of truth comes, he will lead you on the way to the truth. Jesus is the Way, Jesus is the Truth. The Spirit will lead them on the Way to all Truth. What the Spirit does is founded in and on Jesus. He drives us to no destination except to Jesus, who is the truth. Thus even though Jesus was leaving the disciples, yet by the power and working of the Spirit his abiding presence and his truth would never elude them. What Jesus did here was to nicely encourage the disciples to depend on the Spirit of truth.

God is Father, God is Son, God is Spirit. God is Three and God is One. God's oneness is no mere concept. It is oneness in fact and in action. The Father acts through the Son and the Spirit. The Son acts in the Spirit and the Father. The Spirit takes and declares from Jesus everything that belongs to the Father. In the Trinity, there is unity. This same Godhead has made us in his image and likeness. We are meant to be individual persons, living in the image of God's unity. Whenever we allowed social, ethnic, tribal, political, racial, religious, economic or any other differences to mitigate against our unity as a people we vitiated the image of the divine unity which was planted in us at the dawn of creation. Revealing the operations of the Spirit, Jesus also revealed a character of God that could be fostered in us all. With the help of the Spirit, may that unity in God be one day restored wherever and whenever God's children gather.

Come Holy Spirit, fill me with the light of your truth. Kindle in me the fire of your love, that I may be made an instrument of unity, the kind that exists within the Trinity. Never permit that any word, thought or deed of mine will ever be a means of disunity in the midst of your people.

Thursday Of The Sixth Week Of Easter

John 16:16-20

"A little while and you will no longer see me, and
again a little while later and you will see me."

We continue our reflection on Jesus' farewell discourse. The excerpt for our deliberations today is John 16:16-20. In this piece Jesus tells his disciples that a little while, they will no longer see him, and again a little while later they will see him. This is because he goes to the Father. Confused as to what he means by "a little while and a little while later," the disciples started wondering among themselves as what he meant by a little while. One would expect that if the little while was the disciples' problem, Jesus should have explained that to them. He however answers their question saying, "Amen, amen, I say to you, you will weep and mourn, while the world rejoices; you will grieve, but your grief will become joy." This does not seem the right answer to persons who are seeking meaning to "a little while". However, let's reconstruct the flow of Jesus' statements:

- A little while you will never see me
- A little while again you will see me
- Because I go to the Father

The first question is: why will they not see him? Because he goes to the Father. How does he go to the Father? By dying on the Cross. If Jesus dies on the Cross and is buried, obviously the disciples will never see him. The

Passion and the cross is pain not only to Jesus but also to the disciples. The whole experience of the agony in the garden, the betrayal, the abuse of power and denial of justice, the spittle on him, the scourging at the pillar, the crowning with thorns, the carrying of the cross, the denial and abandonment of his friends and ultimately dying on the Cross, will bring actual pain not only to Jesus but any true disciple of his. As they bore their master's pain, the world, thinking they had it all right would laugh to scorn. The disciples would thus grieve as the world rejoiced.

The other question is: Why will they see him again? Because he goes to the Father. How does he go to the Father? He goes to the Father through his Resurrection and Ascension. If any Christ event would be a source of joy, it is the Resurrection. In the Resurrection Christ makes himself manifest to his disciples. He appears to them again and in a little while he who had been dead and buried was seen once again. At the time, they had not left the shock and the grief of his parting and it is in that little while that their tears turned into joy. From the mountain of the Ascension we are told they returned to Jerusalem with joy. Thus once again, they see him go to the Father and their grief turns into joy.

The interesting fact is that Jesus did not say that their grief would go away or fade into thin air. He said that their grief will become joy. The grief is not taken away. It becomes joy. That he combined the two "little whiles" and explained it away with the transition of pain into joy suggests a lesson to the disciples. Pain and joy will always exist. The mystery of the Cross, the Resurrection, and Ascension will always involve pain which becomes joy, lasting joy. B. Wilcoxon states this idea unequivocally when he said, "The good news of Easter does not erase the suffering of the cross, but it does transform it, as it transforms all of creation. The resurrected Jesus still bears the scars on his hands and his side. Pain is a reality, but the pain will be turned into joy."

Friends, today we are asked to model our lives to the mystery of the Lord's Cross. As the way to the Father, it will certainly bring us pain but the joy of the Lord's resurrection and Ascension will always be our strength. When pain comes into our lives and the Lord's yoke doesn't seem as light as he promised, let us remember that he whom the disciples did not see in a little while will in a little while again be seen and all pain will be turned into joy.

My Jesus, your Cross teaches me that pain is a reality, but your Resurrection and Ascension turn pain into joy. May I never shy away from taking up my own cross daily to follow you. And when the pain of the Cross becomes a burden too heavy for me to bear, may your grace accord me some joy to balance my afflictions.

FRIDAY OF THE SIXTH WEEK OF EASTER

John 16:20-23

" I say to you, you will weep and mourn…; you
will grieve, but your grief will become joy."

What are your pains in this pandemic season? What cross do you carry
today?

The other day, I saw on TV a crowd protesting the lockdown in their
community. Among the placards they bore, one of them read, "Covid-19
is not killing us. Unemployment is."

As to whether they are right in assuming that COVID is not killing
them, I will leave it to their own assessment. However, the truth remains
that this pandemic has certainly brought untold hardships to the entire
world. So much has changed and many people around the world are living
in perpetual grief and pain. The fear of the unknown, the uncertainty
surrounding what one is likely to get as one steps out to get the essentials
of life. The limit to our freedoms, the mass loss of dear lives, businesses
and livelihoods, the lack of access to public social functions and religious
observances, forced closure of our schools, strangers locked down in
foreign places they never intended to stay beyond a certain time, the
need to social distance and treat one another like biblical lepers, and the
painful adjustments and readjustments we all have to make in order to
stay safe in the face of a concealed enemy, all bring us discomfort, pain
and grief. People have fallen into depression and some have ended their

lives prematurely. Domestic violence is said to be on the rise and many a parent who has to work from home and also homeschool kids suffers gravely from role tension. We have all had to bear this Cross of grief and pain without knowing when it will go away. Friends and relatives with preexisting conditions have had to live with dread every day. Frontline workers put their own lives and safety and those of their families at risk as they care for the sick. Yet it is in such strange circumstances we find ourselves that Jesus' words come across as our consolation: " I say to you, you will weep and mourn...; you will grieve, but your grief will become joy." He describes our current state of life to that of a woman in travail. She suffers and grieves. However, when she holds her child in her arms, her joy returns again. She no longer remembers the pain because of her joy that a child has been born into the world. So this cross we bear, this cup we drink, will certainly pass us by and the reality of our pain will yield to the joy that will never be taken away from us.

But Jesus says three important things that suggest the source of our lasting joy:

- I will see you again and your hearts will rejoice
- You will not question me about anything
- Whatever you ask the Father in my name he will give you.

Our pain becomes joy because Jesus sees us. Our pain becomes joy not because we question and ask Jesus to turn things around for us but because he takes the initiative to make things right and beautiful on his own and in his own time.

Much as he transforms our pain into lasting joy on his own account and in his own time, he also draws our attention to the need to stay connected to the Father, remaining steadfast in prayer; payer made through his name. As we bear our crosses, we are assured that Jesus will turn an eye to see us again and his gaze will bring us joy. Nonetheless, our vocation to pray unceasingly and keep the live line with the Father through Jesus must also be in vogue: "Amen, amen, I say to you, whatever you ask the Father in my name he will give you."

Yes, Jesus will see us again; yes, Jesus will act in his own time and make things right. Yet in the midst of all these, we will do well to take everything to God in the daily prayer we make in Jesus' name.

My Jesus, the times are difficult and we need you to let your face shine again on us. Kindly spare our world the light of your face and bring us back to salvation even as we ask the Father for healing and restoration in your name.

Saturday Of The Sixth Week Of Easter

John 16:23b-28

"For the Father himself loves you."

We reflect still on Jesus' farewell discourse. Our excerpt is from John 16:23b-28.

One of the early messages that St. John the Evangelist carries across to his audiences is on God's love for the world. According to him it was so much because of God's love for the world that he sent his only begotten Son so that all who believe in him will not perish but have everlasting life. Elsewhere he says that the way we know the love of God is to believe in the one whom he has sent. In the final moments of his parting discourse, Jesus encourages his disciples to ask in his name. He assures them that the Father will do all they asked for in his name. God's answer to their prayer is not because Jesus would plead their cause but because the Father himself loves them. The Father loves them because they love Jesus and believe in him.

God loves us. In his love he grants the prayers we make in Jesus' name to make our joy complete. God loves. He loves us because we love and believe in His Son.

Today, we want to underline 2 things:

- The Father answers our prayer
- The Father himself loves us

It is sometimes difficult to believe in the power of prayer. Other times, praying hardly makes sense. Does God really answer our prayer? The simple answer is Yes. At all times he hears our prayer. The important thing here is to pray steadfastly and in the name of Jesus. Praying in Jesus' name is not just in repeating a formula to suggest that one is making a prayer through Christ our Lord. It is about loving Jesus, believing in him, and thereby living in God's love. The love of God, therefore, is the first condition of answered prayer. If I don't find fulfillment in prayer I need to check my love for Jesus and the extent of my belief in him. If I have a deficit in my love of him, if my faith in him is just skin deep, my prayer to God might be mere babbling and my babbling will only be empty words. St. James once said that we pray but do not receive because our motives are all wrong. The motive with which we go to prayer also underscores the condition for which our prayer should be answered. If the Father loves us He will certainly not grant that which we ask for with a wrong motive. Plato opines that it is not just and perhaps not love to give a knife to its rightful owner if he will kill himself with it. He never grants us that which will turn to unleash harm or commit our souls to the fires of hell. When the Father answers the prayer we make in Jesus' name, He does so to bring us joy that is complete. The greatest answer to prayer then is the lasting joy that God gives us because we prayed. Whenever we went to prayer with love and faith in the heart, that honest and sincere prayer of ours brings an incomprehensible inner joy, the kind nothing can rob us of. We could be in dire straits, but the grace received from the act of prayer itself feeds our souls so well that we know nothing but inner peace and lasting joy. If then we increase our love for Jesus, if we step up our belief in Him, we will bask in the Father's love and the prayer of faith we do with the right motive, in the name of Jesus, will be granted us by the Father who knows what is best and what would bring us abiding joy.

The Father himself loves you. Has there ever been a moment in life that we have been tempted to either question or doubt God's love? Sometimes life becomes a hell. All we touch turns sour. Every endeavor of ours falls flat. Life is emptied of meaning and despair is the food we eat. The Psalmist was in such a situation when he cried, "How long o Lord? Will you forget me forever? How long must I bear this grief in my soul, this sorrow in my heart all day? How long shall my enemy prevail over me?" Perhaps we have all come into such moments before when our God seemed very distant, loveless, and deaf to our pleas. Today, Jesus emphatically reassures us of the Father's love: For the Father himself loves you. When life becomes a bed of thorns, when the shadows fall, we should never be discouraged. On the Cross Jesus cried, Eloi, Eloi, lama sabachthani, but His Father never abandoned him to the netherworld. He raised him up on the third day and received him into His glory. Just as the Father loves the Son, He loves us too and He will never abandon us to our fate. Every day, let us think of the love the Father has for us, by letting us be called God's children. He loves us because we love and believe in his Son.

My Jesus, love of you, and faith in you open me up to your Father's love. May your grace increase your love and faith in me so that living in your Father's love, my daily spiritual exercises will bring me lasting joy. May the love of your Father surround me today and all the days of my life.

THE ASCENSION OF THE LORD

Heaven made Real

"...as they were looking on, he was lifted up,
and a cloud took him from their sight."

Msgr. Arthur Tonne tells the story of a boy whose family name was Carpenter. The Carpenters lived in a remote mountainous village all their lives and never really traveled beyond the confines of their microcosm. If they knew any place better, it was their immediate surroundings and nothing more. As a teenager, Carpenter's father took him on his first trip to the city. There, he saw paved streets, skyscrapers, and electricity for the first time. The boy wanted to stay there and get an education. His father arranged for him to board with some family friends, who generously financed his studies when he decided to become a doctor. He graduated with honors but declined all job offers to practice medicine in the city. He opted to go back to the mountains, where there were many sick people and few doctors.

For many years he ministered to the sick. Some paid, most couldn't. He gave his very best and helped everyone he could. In his old age, he was in broken health himself and almost penniless. Two small rooms above the town grocery store were his home and office. At the foot of the creaky stairs leading up to his office was a sign with these words: "Dr. Carpenter is upstairs." One morning someone climbed those stairs to find the devoted doctor dead. The entire community was plunged in grief. They wanted to erect some kind of monument to him. However, they decided to simply write these words on a large tombstone: "Dr. Carpenter is upstairs."

Friends this week, we celebrate the solemnity of the Ascension. This feast simply has to say that Jesus the Divine Doctor of our souls is "upstairs" in Heaven, where he ascended after his Resurrection. He has ascended to make heaven accessible to all and sundry. Christ is in heaven not as if he is on some other planet distinct from ours. Rather he has entered into a new level of life where his human face makes an appearance in divine intimacy with the father. We profess in the Creed that Jesus Christ was crucified, he died and was buried; that he descended into the dead, rose again on the third day and ascended into heaven; and is seated at the right hand of God the Father. So at the Father's right hand, Jesus lives in communion with the Father. From there he sees and assists us always. He has not disappeared from us, neither has he abandoned us. He has rather made the Father's house and God's life and happiness accessible to mankind and offered our human nature to the Father. He has reinforced our hope and confidence that where he is, we shall also be (see CCC 661). He himself reassured us that after having gone to prepare a place for us, he shall come and take us so where he is, we shall also be.

Ascension is thus one feast that should set our minds on things of heaven. It is the feast that should set our gaze on the heavenly places and reinforce our hopes in life yet to come. It is the feast that reassures us that there is a home in view, a home where Jesus has taken up his place in his glory. E. Vaughan composed a song on heaven as our final prize. In that beautiful song, the composer wrote that, Yes, Heaven is the prize; My soul shall strive to gain. One glimpse of Paradise Repays a life of pain. 'T is Heaven; yes heaven. Yes, heaven is the prize; 'T is Heaven, 't is Heaven. Yes, heaven is the prize.

Every Christian lives their lives with heaven in view. All our hopes, faith, and love aim at obtaining the heavenly inheritance. In all the many dangers, toils and snares in life, our hope conquers our pain and lights the way; and even when our hope dies along the way, our faith shows the crown and our love continues to reign because heaven looms as our ultimate prize.

Christ, who alone can make heaven accessible to us, has left his footprints in the rocks as he ascended into heaven. Without abandoning us, he has led the way and has left us the trail of his footprints so that we can follow him to everlasting life. His going up is like the rising of incense. Quinn and Griffin opined that as Catholics, the wistful trails of the smoke of the incense we use in our ceremonies are symbolic of ourselves. As we watch the smoke rise, we pray that somehow, someday, we would, like Jesus, be caught up in the clouds, and rising, reach the eternal God whom we acknowledge as our Father. Thus just as Jesus was lifted in the clouds to the father, and just as the clouds of the incense ascend to God, we, at the end of this life hope to make it upstairs to be with God.

Indeed our gaze must be on heavenly realms. Yet we must not be caught unawares, neither should we be left gazing in a state of inertia, fixing our eyes on the heavens as if there is no hope, and no faith. When the disciples were caught in such an unfortunate state, the angel had to remind them that there was no need for them to keep fixing their gaze into the skies. That Jesus whom they saw ascending would come the same way they saw him go. This is why, as we seek the things above, Jesus continues to be present to us and is eager to help us through the Sacraments, the Bible, and the Church. We, on our part, joyfully go about our Master's business, spreading his kingdom, doing good, eschewing evil, and staying connected to him in our humble prayers. Every time we turn to Him in prayer, we climb the stairs to his office. Because he is upstairs, Dr. Jesus is always powerfully upstairs, seated at his Father's right hand as our Mediator, Savior, and King.

My Jesus, as you take your place at your Father's right hand, may you send forth the Spirit to kindle in us the fire of your love in our hearts. Let your Spirit heal our world and create it anew for your great glory.

Monday Of The Seventh Week Of Easter

John 16:29-33

"In the world you will have trouble, but take
courage, I have conquered the world."

Today we reflect on the tail end of Jesus' farewell discourse. In John 16:29-
33, the disciples have a clear view of Jesus' discourse. They are happy to
acknowledge their comprehension of all he taught, to acknowledge the
authority behind his teaching and the fruit of Jesus' teaching. "Now we
know that you have come from God, you know everything and you need
no one to question you. Because of this, we have come to believe."

Now, if I come to know and believe in a person who is God-sent, any
adversity befalling that person might completely destroy me. Jesus, knew
this. He also knew what was about to happen to him. He knew the possible
repercussions his passion and death would have on the disciples who had
come to believe. He, therefore, took it upon himself to open their eyes to
the reality: indeed you have come to believe, yet very soon the world would
do its worst to me and you will all scatter and abandon me. The truth is
that if that happens because the Father is with me I will never be alone.
I am telling you this so that when it happens you will have peace in me.
"In the world, you will have trouble, but take courage, I have conquered
the world."

A number of things happen in this piece:

- Jesus' teaching brings knowledge to the disciples.
- Jesus' teaching leads them to belief
- Jesus exposes them to the impending reality
- Jesus gives them a reassurance of his peace.
- Jesus gifts them with courage and victory over the troubles of the world.

The word of God never falls without leading to knowledge. Whenever God's word falls, God has something new to teach his people. The disciples after following the farewell discourse came to know Jesus as the one who came down from heaven. By virtue of our own baptism, we have been made bearers of God's word. Our first duty is to draw knowledge and understanding from his word. Having been so informed, our next duty is to live what we have known in such a way that our lives would be an open bible for others to read and come to know God. In our relationships, our lives need to be discourses that will impart knowledge of God to others. God makes knowledge of himself available to others through my godly conduct.

The word of God also leads to faith. Following the farewell discourse, the disciples came to believe that Jesus came down from the Father. Jesus lives in you. Jesus lives in me. He delivers his daily discourses to his people through us. If others would come to the faith in him, it sometimes depends on you and me. When Gandhi fell in love with Jesus and entertained the desire to taste Christianity, it took the conduct of Christians to drive him away from the faith. The stories we tell as Christians with our day to day conduct, go a long way to either inspire faith or discourage faith in others.

Jesus knew his disciples. He knew what would befall them on account of his passion and death. He knew their conduct in response to his passion would rob them of inner peace. So he got real with them but also assured them of peace in him. He anticipated their falling but prevented their inner self-destruction by promising them peace. In the dark world of sin and strife, the love of God continues to whisper peace within us. Let us hear his words of peace again today, "I have told you this so that you might have peace in me."

Sometimes we seem to have lost control over our world. We feel this way because we try to live our life without Jesus. The truth is that life lived devoid of Jesus brings nothing but trouble and pain. Like the biblical people of Babel, we try to build towers by ourselves and for ourselves only to behold them collapse and confuse our language. In the midst of all the troubles we see, our strength and courage are in the Lord Jesus. He is true and his promises are true. What he says to his disciples he says to us too, "In the world, you will have trouble, but take courage, I have conquered the world."

My Jesus, I take my place at thy feet to savor and meditate on the sweetness of your word. May I be so imbued with the knowledge of you that my conduct will inspire in others knowledge and faith in you. In this world's troubles may the power of your hand which conquers all infuse peace in my heart and accord me the courage I need to carry through.

TUESDAY OF THE SEVENTH WEEK OF EASTER

John 17:1-11

"Jesus raised his eyes to heaven."

Today, we begin reading from the 17th chapter of John.

One thing St. John the Evangelist did not do in his Gospel was to narrate the story of the Last Supper. What he rather does is to tell the details of some of the events that took place in the Upper Room. From chapter 13 to 16, the Evangelist presents Jesus' washing of the disciples' feet and the lesson of brotherly love that ensued. He then went through the details of Jesus' farewell discourse until the end of chapter 16.

In chapter 17, Jesus transitions from teaching to prayer. The farewell discourse gives room for his priestly prayer. Matthew Henry underscores the strategic positioning of Jesus' prayer in the structure of John's gospel. Until this time the Passover meal was done. From this point on Jesus was going to go the way of the Cross. Of what significance then is his prayer? His prayer is significant because:

- It is said after the farewell discourse
- It is said after the Passover meal
- It is said before the passion
- It is said in a family setting

The farewell discourse of Jesus was a kind of a homily or a sermon he gave his disciples. In the discourse, he revealed some of the mysteries of the Godhead to them. He allayed their fears and gifted them with peace and courage. He also promised them the Advocate. In effect he empowered them to live a meaningful life. It was after this enlightenment, it was after this sermon that Jesus prayed. When we have offered pieces of advice, when we have taught another to live a meaningful life, when we have empowered others to grow in faith, when we have taught our children to choose the right way, do we also take time to pray with them and for them?

It was a prayer Jesus said after the Passover meal. If we take the Passover meal for a family reunion, it was a prayer said to conclude such a reunion. If this Last Supper is also the institution of the Eucharist, then it was a prayer after the Eucharist. Many a time, we have our family convocations and reunions. How often have we begun such reunions and ended them with prayer? And when we come to the Eucharist, do we see the end of it as an opportunity for prayer? Often we are in a rush to go to other businesses and we miss that golden opportunity to raise our eyes to the heavens in a prayer of adoration and thanksgiving to Jesus who has come to dwell in our hearts.

It was a prayer said before the passion and the death of Jesus. The Last Supper and the crucifixion are intrinsically bound together. When Jesus took bread and said, "this is my flesh," when he took the wine and said "this is my blood, " he prefigured the sacrifice on the Cross. The prayer he said before going to the cross is a prayer before the sacrifice. Christ, therefore, did not only pray after the sacrifice, he also prayed before the sacrifice. Whenever we meet to offer the sacrifice of the Eucharist, we need to prepare ourselves in prayer. Sometimes this demands that we show up a little early to put ourselves in a prayerful disposition before the solemn sacrifice begins. Other times it demands that we observe our quiet times, prayerfully reflect on the word of God to be broken in the Eucharist and dispose ourselves to receive Jesus who offers himself for us on the Cross. In our own little sacrifices, we make in life, it is important that we take time to pray about them before and after we make them. Parents make lots of sacrifices for their families every day. I am wondering how often they talk to God about these sacrifices. Many of us spend ourselves for the benefit and comfort of others, how often do we take our sacrifices to God in prayer.

The Passover is a family meal. If Jesus ate it with his disciples, they had at the time constituted one family in Christ. Praying with them and for them, Jesus gave meaning to family prayer. It is said that a family that prays together stays together. Jesus prayed with them to bind them in unity. He did not merely use the art of prayer to unite them, he actually prayed for their unity. We will put our own families on a different spiritual pedestal if we could but find time for the family to gather and pray. Prayer is the fuel that runs the engine of the family and the more the family does it together, the stronger they belong to each other.

Finally, Jesus prayed, raising his eyes to heaven. What did he do? R. B. Young is of the view that raising his eyes to heaven, Jesus looked beyond worldly limits to a far greater, unlimited life. He looked, in prayer, beyond the cross to the resurrection. Friends, this is what we do when we begin our day and endeavors with prayer. This is what we do when we intersperse our life's moments with prayer. This is what we do when we end the day and life's events with prayer. We look beyond our worldly limits and place our trust in the Author of eternal life. When we carry our joys and pains to God in prayer, we look beyond the Cross to the Resurrection. We cement our faith in the One who has power over the ruler of the earth and is able to conquer death with life. Prayer is thus a powerful tool we need to carry with us on this pilgrimage of life.

My Jesus, by the light of your Spirit, teach me to pray as you did. Every day in my life, grant me the grace to look beyond the worldly limits of life, may I never cease to set my gaze beyond the cross and count on you who alone can make my life meaningful.

WEDNESDAY OF THE SEVENTH
WEEK OF EASTER

John 17:11b-19

It was the town's festival Sunday. The church was extraordinarily filled to capacity. Okanta rises to pray: Thank you Lord for this feast. Thank you for the joy it brings. Thank you for the families you bring together. But Lord, I have a problem. Today, as most families are eating sumptuously well, we are starving in my family. Please touch the hearts of all who have it to support the have-nots. Amen. The entire church turned hilarious. Yet Okanta's prayer expressed what was in his heart. This is what prayer does. It pours out and communicates what is in an individual's heart.

Today, Jesus continues to pray for the disciples and we see what's in his heart for them:

- Keep them in your name
- May they be one.
- I protected them and guided them in your name that you gave me.
- None was lost.
- May they share my joy completely
- I gave them your word
- The world hated them because they do not belong to the world.
- Do not take them out of the world but protect them from the evil one.
- Consecrate them in the truth
- As you sent me into the world, so I sent them into the world.
- I consecrate myself for them, so they may be consecrated in the truth.

Each of Jesus' prayer points is very instructive. In fact, they are so instructive that some scholars consider Jesus' entire prayer as an apex to his farewell discourse. I would like to pick and choose from these prayer points and make some remarks:

Keep them in your name. The name of God is God himself. God cannot be distinguished from his name. What he is, is his name. To protect someone in his name is to protect the one in himself. The word Jesus uses here is the same word used in keeping a prisoner. It suggests giving maximum security to the one kept. Thus Jesus prays that God will build a wall around his disciples and wrap his arms around them, keeping them safely and intimately in himself. Such was Jesus' prayer for them, such is his prayer for you and me today. May the Lord keep us in his name.

I protected them in the name that you gave me and none was lost. When we have protection in Jesus, we are so secure that we cannot be lost. We only get lost by the choices we make. Judas was lost because he extracted himself from Jesus' safekeeping. He was lost to selfishness and sin. Let us pray to remain steadfast in the shelter and the embrace of Jesus so nothing will separate us from him.

The world hated them, they did so for two reasons:

a. Because Jesus gave them God's word.
b. Because they do not belong to the world.

The word of God is truth. If the world hated them because Jesus gave them God's word, they were hated because of the truth. Why would the world hate me? What would the world hate you for? Shall we be hated because of the truth or because of deceit? May it never happen that we will attract the world's hatred for any reason but the truth. Our world is thirsting for the truth and if no one will give her the truth, Christians should and we should do so even if doing so will cause the world to hate us.

They were hated also because they did not belong to the world. To belong to the world is to be ruled by worldly standards. To belong to the world is to flow with the world's standards. To belong to the world is to compromise on the side of human weaknesses. However, the true disciple is a challenge to the worldly conscience. He is ruled by virtue and heavenly standards. The law of God is his guiding principle. Today, will the world love me or hate me. If I have to choose between the world and God, whom will I choose?

Keep them in the world but guard them against the evil one. As Christians, we cannot impact the world if we live outside it. We need to be in it to transform it. This does not exonerate us from the wiles of the evil one. One cannot live in the mud without getting muddy. As we remain in the world, trials and temptations will abound. Privations and misfortunes will befall us. We shall rise and fall with the vicissitudes of life. The important thing is that in all these, Satan will not gain the soul that costs so dear. It is thus heartwarming that Jesus prays, admitting the reality of our need to be in the world and at the same time asking for us to be protected from the snares of the ruler of the world.

Truth stands forever. Jesus prays that they be consecrated in the truth. "Consecrate them in the truth." Philosophers think that truth is that which is not open to reasonable debate. All honest thinking beings accept the truth because it is what it is and not what it is not. Truth is universal. Truth is necessary, it depends on no other to manifest itself. It is appropriate everywhere and does not demand situational conditions to be what it is. Truth is timeless. It is said to demand no verification and is best communicated by repetition; it is self-evident. Truth is authentic, simple, and guileless, lacking all duplicity.

To consecrate is to make or declare something sacred. When Christ prayed that they be consecrated in the truth, he prayed that they be made constantly, transparently, and consistently true in holiness. He prayed that they are made authentically holy, sacred by all standards. That their holy lives be devoid of duplicity and deceit. Jesus, the Truth, who consecrated himself for our sake is the same yesterday, today, and forever. His prayer is that what we authentically are in sanctity, we should forever be and what we are must be as self-evident as the truth is. Whoever makes an encounter with us must thus encounter the truth that Jesus is. Whoever deals with us must deal with the truth incarnate and not with an epitome of deceit.

Come, Holy Spirit. Keep us in the name the Father gave to the Son. Consecrate us in the truth. Even when we incur the world's displeasure on account of the truth we bear, may your grace in us increase so that your truth will stand forever for the salvation of the world.

Thursday Of The Seventh Week Of Easter

John 17:20-26

Jesus prayed saying:

"I pray not only for these, but also for those who will believe in me through their word, so that they may all be one..."

As we continue our reflection on Jesus' priestly prayer, we underline the following prayer points of his:

- I pray for those who will come to believe in me through their word.
- May they be one as you are in me and I in you.
- I have given them the glory you gave me, that they may be one.
- May they be brought to perfection as one.
- So that the world may know that you sent me, and you love them even as you loved me.
- They are your gift to me.
- I wish that where I am they also will be with me.
- The world does not know you but I know you and they know that I came from you.
- I made your name known. I will make it known to them so that your love for me will be in them and I will be in them.

It is interesting to see that Jesus prays for the fruits of the future ministry of his disciples. He prays not only for the disciples but also for those who would come to believe in him through their proclamation of the word. After the Resurrection he would send them out to make disciples of all nations, baptizing in the name of the Trinity. Yet even before that event, he prays for those who would come to believe. He anticipates in prayer, the success of their future mission. The practice is good in which Christians pray not only about current issues and successes but also about the not yet.

One of the things we were asked to pray about as seminarians were the priest(s) we would work with in the future, especially in the early hours of our ministry. At the time, it made little sense to me but faithfully I did so as often as I could. However, experience has taught me that it was an intention worth praying for, as I have grown to realize that the encounters we make at the early hours of ministry can either make or unmake the priesthood of a newly ordained. Praying about the future of the ventures we make, praying for the future of our work, praying about yet to be made acquaintances, praying for the future of our kids, and for the future spouses of our kids, praying for the unknown people we would have to deal with someday, the unknown dangers we are likely to face, the joys we shall see, the successes to be chalked, our future failures and many more are things for us to consider today. If we have a dream, it is worthwhile to commit it to prayer, asking for God's will to be done. Much as tomorrow takes care of itself, it is important to lift our tomorrows into God's hands and ask him to order our future aright and steer the moments of our lives toward his own ends and purposes. God holds the future. He alone can fix it even when we screw it. Let's entrust him with ours.

If anything was important to Jesus in his followers, it was the love and unity that needed to exist among them. He did not only wish unity among his immediate disciples but also those who would later come to believe. He made the unity and love between him and the Father an ideal exemplar for emulation. Just as the Father is in him and he is in the Father, Jesus wants us to be one in him and with one another. Unfortunately in his name, families continue to live in disunity. Christian denominations live in suspicion and abuse of each other. The call for ecumenism sometimes appears only as a euphemism for seeming peaceful coexistence. True love, true unity continue to be a dream for many a family and many a follower of

Jesus. Jesus' prayer is that we become one just as he is one with the Father. His wish is that we dwell with him wherever he is. I am wondering how it would look like when after all our ideological wars, after having lived like cats and dogs here on earth, we all end up where Jesus is. Having failed to see eye to eye with each other here on earth, will we have the courage to look at each other in the eyes later in the sight of Jesus?

We are all gifts God has made to his Son. We are precious to God. Jesus holds us dearly to his heart. He so loves us that he never wants to part with us. His greatest wish is to have us with him wherever he is. He wants to fold his arms around us and stay his gaze on us. He wraps us every day with the bond of love that exists between him and the Father. This is why he made the Father's name known to us. This is why continues to make the Father's name known to us so that God's love will be in us and Jesus will dwell in us. Have I embraced God's name as revealed in Christ Jesus his Son? God's name is God. In God, name and identity coincide. What God is, is God's name. When Jesus revealed the Father's name, it is the Father himself that he revealed. Knowing his name is knowing Him. Do I know God? Is God the ruler of my life? Do I acknowledge God in my initiatives? Do I give him the prominence he deserves in my life?

My Jesus, I lift my future into your hands. May your Spirit step ahead of me to order it the way you want it. Grant that in the spirit of love and unity I will walk hand in hand with all I encounter with respect and mutual trust. Your Father has given me to you as a gift, guard me as the apple of your eye, and unite my heart to acknowledge his name as you reveal him to me every day.

FRIDAY OF THE SEVENTH WEEK OF EASTER

John 21:15-17

"Simon, son of John, do you love me more than these?" Simon Peter answered him, "Yes, Lord, you know that I love you."

We reflect today on an aspect of the epilogue of the gospel of John. In chapter 21, the disciples return with Peter to their former way of life. They were fishermen when Jesus called them, now they make a return to the very same trade and the spot where it all began: the Sea of Galilee. When they failed in their all-night fishing venture, Jesus directs them to a miraculous catch. At the shore, he serves them breakfast and no one dared to ask of his identity because they knew who he was. If they knew who he was, what went on in Peter's mind apart from diving into the sea to shield his nakedness? Should he not have captured the opportunity of the miraculous catch and breakfast to right the wrongs of his threefold denial of Jesus? If he saw the need, did he want to take the chance and make amends, or was he struggling with the thought of his denial? What would Jesus do after he had been so badly denied?

In John 13, Peter promised his unflinching support to Jesus. If all abandoned Jesus, he would never do so. He would even die for Jesus. Not quite long after, he denied Jesus three times and did so even under oath. Today, he makes an encounter with Jesus and Jesus takes the initiative to restore their relationship.

Three times Jesus would ask: Simon, son of Jonah do you love me? The questions gradually turn so intense and rather emotional that Peter begins to hurt within. You know everything, Lord. You know I love you. Three times, he charged him to feed and tend the sheep and the lambs. Finally, Jesus asked Peter to follow him.

As I read today's gospel, my mind is drawn to how we restore broken relationships. My question is: Must hurts always lead to confrontations? And, Is it all right to hurt another and sweep it under the carpet because we love them and we know they know we do?

To me, this reading, among others, suggests that we must not ignore the hurts we bring to others. Neither should any attempt to restore a wounded relationship end in bitter confrontations and a sour ending.

Three times, Peter badly denied his Master. He knew he did wrong. He was embarrassed by it. From his response to Jesus, he knew that Jesus knew of his love for Jesus. However, Jesus' knowledge of Peter's genuine love for him wouldn't be a reason to ignore the fact that Peter acted below the dignity of a true friend. In fact, their friendship had been so profoundly wounded, that Jesus would desist from affectionately calling him Cephas. He would rather call him Simon, son of Jonah, the name he had when they first met. Yet all Jesus did was to give Peter the chance to live above his shame, renew his love for Jesus, and demonstrate that love by tending the lambs and feeding the sheep. The idea is that Peter could not take it for granted that Jesus' knowledge of his love for him should be enough to let life continue as if nothing went wrong. However, that which needed to be addressed to restore a broken relationship was done amicably and in the means of love. See what Jesus did: He helped Peter when he failed in his fishing venture. He set a table for Peter and his friends. Then he nicely welled up Peter's love for him as a means of restoring him to be the pastor he had always meant him to be. He restored Peter without any confrontations and without any reference to or mention of his past offenses. Could Jesus have scolded Peter for denying him and also initiating a return to the fishing business? Yes! Yet, all he did was to give love a fighting chance to enable Peter to shepherd his flock.

Friends, we live in a world of fragile peace and broken promises. Times are when we fail to meet expectations in our relationships. We fail our friends and betray them. We hurt and are hurt intentionally and otherwise. Sometimes our conduct brings us embarrassment and embarrassment robs us of the courage to do the right thing. Other times we rely on the presumed knowledge and understanding of the other and think that life can go on without necessarily addressing the mistakes. On the flip side of the coin, we tend to know only one way to conflict resolution- ie, bitter confrontation. The encounter of Peter and Jesus today opens our eyes to the fact that like Peter, we can deny the master, like Peter, we can betray each other's trust, but unlike Peter, it should not be too difficult to seize the opportunity to patch up. We should never ignore the roots to strained relationships. Life must not continue when the air has not been cleared. Nevertheless, like Jesus, even when we have been hurt, love must be the means to resolution. Sometimes we need to anticipate the difficulty of the erring party and create a conducive platform for the process of forgiveness to begin. So much is achieved when broken relationships are fixed. Peter led the church. He gave up his life as a witness to the gospel. His witness to Jesus was the kind that not even death could erase. He died for the glory of God. He loved Jesus and he lived it to the full. Such love couldn't have been wasted away because of his earlier denial of his master.

My Jesus, while I was still a sinner, you died to save me. Yet I continue daily to wallow in sin. May your love always give me the grace to make amends for my sins and may that same love bring me your forgiveness so that in spite of my weaknesses I will still live my life as a living witness to your love.

Saturday Of The Seventh Week Of Easter

John 21:20-25

When Peter saw him, he said to Jesus, "Lord, what about him?"

We read today the tail end of John's Gospel

Having been forgiven, restored as to pasture the sheep, and to follow Jesus till he would die in witness to God's glory, Peter turns to see the Beloved Disciple. He inquired of Jesus, "What about him?" Did he inquire out of genuine concern about the future of this disciple or out of jealousy as is sometimes opined? Jesus' rather strange answer was, "What if I want him to remain until I come? What concern is it of yours? You follow me." Strangely enough, Jesus' statement was misconstrued to mean that the Beloved Disciple shall never die. This is the word that the media reported around the world. However, he who reported the life story of Jesus as we have read, wrote what he witnessed as his testimony is true. What he committed to writing was only a fraction of all that Jesus did and taught. For Jesus accomplished so much as no book on earth could contain.

Let's underline the following:

- Peter's inquiry on John
- Jesus' response to the inquiry
- Jesus' response misconstrued and mispresented
- John's true testimony.

"Lord, what about him?" As I skim through comments made on this inquiry of Peter, I am inclined to believe that he asked this question out of jealousy. My wonder is how Peter would be jealous of John after all the experiences they had made together till this point. Indeed Jesus had just predicted Peter's martyrdom but if Peter had been so forgiven and restored to pasture the sheep he should have no reason to envy any of the others in the fold. Having been entrusted with much, his primary concern should be to stay focused, follow the Master, and trust him to take care of all the others. This, I think is exactly what Jesus communicated when he said in reply, "What if I want him to remain until I come? What concern is it of yours? You follow me." In my view, Peter's question was borne more out of genuine concern and interest in a friend's future wellbeing than of jealousy. However, his laudable affection and interest in John were misplaced as it would distract him from following Jesus as he had just been asked to do. Sometimes, our genuine interest and affection for others could prevent our trust in Jesus' ability to deliver in their lives.

Other times we worry unnecessarily about other people's future wellbeing when we need to trust that our God has a plan for everyone and his will is surely going to be done in their lives. It is even possible that if we remained faithful in our own individual vocations we could offer up our dedicated services and sacrifices to God for the wellbeing of the people we care so much about. This is why I think the most important thing Peter needed to know at the time was not what Jesus willed for the Beloved Disciple but rather Peter's own focus and fidelity to his call to follow Jesus.

It very often happens that people want to hear things they want to hear. It is also the case that sensationalism tends to appeal more to the human ear than the truth. For this reason, many people easily fall prey to the temptation of telling others what they want to hear. This is a phenomenon that has influenced the dissemination of information in our world until today.

Take a peek at today's news reportage and you will wonder where the truth really lies. We are good at hearing what other people do and say the way we want it and reporting it accordingly. Accuracy with its attendant total truths in information dissemination is usually zero. What did Jesus say to Peter? "What if I want him to remain until I come?" Then word spread among the brothers that the disciple would not die. However, the word that went around was not exactly what Jesus said. People reported what Jesus said and decided to forget everything he said. For those reporters, sensationalism was better than the whole truth. They, therefore, eliminated the early part of Jesus' answer and spread the rest which only suggested that John would not die. This attitude is contrasted with what John himself did after he witnessed the life of Jesus and gave testimony to it. In his own words, "It is this disciple who testifies to these things and has written them, and we know that his testimony is true." Unlike those who reported Jesus' response to Peter, John witnessed and gave a true testimony to the life of Christ.

Our world sometimes bleeds because so much falsehood is sold out to the general public. For various reasons, it is very easy for someone's innocent act or statement to be twisted and employed for mischief. I believe our world would be a better home if the culture and the practice of spewing half-baked truths would give way to nothing but the truth, truth as is witnessed in the testimony of the beloved disciple.

My Jesus, like Peter, you have called me to follow you. May I focus on my vocation and in truth, diligently sacrifice myself in your service. May every sacrifice of mine be acceptable in your sight as an offering I make for the wellbeing of all my friends.

REFERENCE LIST

Bartunek, J. (2014). *The better part: A Christ-centered resource for personal prayer.* Clayton, NC: Ministry23.

Benedict, & Cameron, P. J. (2007). *Benedictus: Day by day with Pope Benedict XVI.* Yonkers, NY: Magnificat.

Brown, R. E., Fitzmyer, J. A., & Murphy, R. E. (2014). *The new Jerome biblical commentary.* London: Bloomsbury.

Catechism of the Catholic Church. (1994). London, England: Geoffrey Chapman.

Crowley, J. A. (1990). *A day with the Lord.* Huntington, IN: Our Sunday Visitor Pub. Division, Our Sunday Visitor.

EPriest.com / Best Practices and Homily Resources for ... (n.d.). Retrieved February-May 2020, from https://www.epriest.com

Fuller, R. C., Johnston, L., Kearns, C., & Orchard, B. (1975). *A New Catholic commentary on holy scripture.* London: Nelson.

Hurd, R. S. (2012). The living gospel: Daily devotions for Lent 2013. Ave Maria Press.

Jarvis, C. A., & Johnson, E. E. (2014). *Feasting on the Gospels.* Louisville, KY: Westminster John Knox Press.

Henry, Matthew. Matthew Henry's Commentary on the Whole Bible. Peabody, MA: Hendrickson, 2009.

Rawlins, C. L., & Barclay, W. (1978). *The Daily study Bible series, revised edition William Barclay: all volumes.* Philadelphia: Westminster Press.

Thomas, & Kimball, P. M. (2012). *Commentary on the Gospel of St. Matthew.* U.S.?: Dolorosa Press.

Thomas, A. (2010). *Catena aurea, commentary on the four gospels.* Place of publication not identified: Nabu Press.

Tonne, A. (1977). *Five minute homilies on the Gospels of cycles A, B, C: (every homily begins with a story).*

ABOUT THE AUTHOR

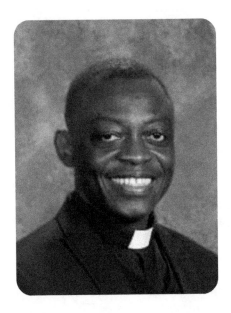

Rev. Fr. Joseph Okine-Quartey (Ph.D.), was ordained in 1996. He has served the greater part of his priestly life as a seminary professor. He has also served as a chaplain at the University of Ghana and the Ghana Parliament House. He is currently the pastor of St. John the Baptist, Plum City, WI, and St. Joseph, Arkansaw, WI. He is also the Dean for the Durand Deanery of the diocese of La Crosse, WI, USA.